PAROLE, DESISTANCE from CRIME, and COMMUNITY INTEGRATION

Committee on Community Supervision and Desistance from Crime

Committee on Law and Justice

Division of Behavioral and Social Sciences and Education

NATIONAL RESEARCH COUNCIL
OF THE NATIONAL ACADEMIES

THE NATIONAL ACADEMIES PRESS
Washington, D.C.
www.nap.edu

THE NATIONAL ACADEMIES PRESS   500 Fifth Street, N.W.   Washington, DC 20001

NOTICE: The project that is the subject of this report was approved by the Governing Board of the National Research Council, whose members are drawn from the councils of the National Academy of Sciences, the National Academy of Engineering, and the Institute of Medicine. The members of the committee responsible for the report were chosen for their special competences and with regard for appropriate balance.

This study was supported by a contract between the National Academy of Sciences and the National Institute of Justice. Any opinions, findings, conclusions, or recommendations expressed in this publication are those of the author(s) and do not necessarily reflect the views of the organizations or agencies that provided support for the project.

International Standard Book Number-13: 978-309-11081-5
International Standard Book Number-10: 0-309-11081-5

Additional copies of this report are available from the National Academies Press, 500 Fifth Street, N.W., Lockbox 285, Washington, DC 20055; (800) 624-6242 or (202) 334-3313 (in the Washington metropolitan area); Internet http://www.nap.edu.

Printed in the United States of America.

Copyright 2008 by the National Academy of Sciences. All rights reserved.

Suggested citation: National Research Council. (2008). *Parole, Desistance from Crime, and Community Integration.* Committee on Community Supervision and Desistance from Crime. Committee on Law and Justice, Division of Behavioral and Social Sciences and Education. Washington, DC: The National Academies Press.

THE NATIONAL ACADEMIES
Advisers to the Nation on Science, Engineering, and Medicine

The **National Academy of Sciences** is a private, nonprofit, self-perpetuating society of distinguished scholars engaged in scientific and engineering research, dedicated to the furtherance of science and technology and to their use for the general welfare. Upon the authority of the charter granted to it by the Congress in 1863, the Academy has a mandate that requires it to advise the federal government on scientific and technical matters. Dr. Ralph J. Cicerone is president of the National Academy of Sciences.

The **National Academy of Engineering** was established in 1964, under the charter of the National Academy of Sciences, as a parallel organization of outstanding engineers. It is autonomous in its administration and in the selection of its members, sharing with the National Academy of Sciences the responsibility for advising the federal government. The National Academy of Engineering also sponsors engineering programs aimed at meeting national needs, encourages education and research, and recognizes the superior achievements of engineers. Dr. Charles M. Vest is president of the National Academy of Engineering.

The **Institute of Medicine** was established in 1970 by the National Academy of Sciences to secure the services of eminent members of appropriate professions in the examination of policy matters pertaining to the health of the public. The Institute acts under the responsibility given to the National Academy of Sciences by its congressional charter to be an adviser to the federal government and, upon its own initiative, to identify issues of medical care, research, and education. Dr. Harvey V. Fineberg is president of the Institute of Medicine.

The **National Research Council** was organized by the National Academy of Sciences in 1916 to associate the broad community of science and technology with the Academy's purposes of furthering knowledge and advising the federal government. Functioning in accordance with general policies determined by the Academy, the Council has become the principal operating agency of both the National Academy of Sciences and the National Academy of Engineering in providing services to the government, the public, and the scientific and engineering communities. The Council is administered jointly by both Academies and the Institute of Medicine. Dr. Ralph J. Cicerone and Dr. Charles M. Vest are chair and vice chair, respectively, of the National Research Council.

www.national-academies.org

THE NATIONAL ACADEMIES
Advisers to the Nation on Science, Engineering, and Medicine

The **National Academy of Sciences** is a private, nonprofit, self-perpetuating society of distinguished scholars engaged in scientific and engineering research, dedicated to the furtherance of science and technology and to their use for the general welfare. Upon the authority of the charter granted to it by the Congress in 1863, the Academy has a mandate that requires it to advise the federal government on scientific and technical matters. Dr. Ralph J. Cicerone is president of the National Academy of Sciences.

The **National Academy of Engineering** was established in 1964, under the charter of the National Academy of Sciences, as a parallel organization of outstanding engineers. It is autonomous in its administration and in the selection of its members, sharing with the National Academy of Sciences the responsibility for advising the federal government. The National Academy of Engineering also sponsors engineering programs aimed at meeting national needs, encourages education and research, and recognizes the superior achievements of engineers. Dr. Charles M. Vest is president of the National Academy of Engineering.

The **Institute of Medicine** was established in 1970 by the National Academy of Sciences to secure the services of eminent members of appropriate professions in the examination of policy matters pertaining to the health of the public. The Institute acts under the responsibility given to the National Academy of Sciences by its congressional charter to be an adviser to the federal government and, upon its own initiative, to identify issues of medical care, research, and education. Dr. Harvey V. Fineberg is president of the Institute of Medicine.

The **National Research Council** was organized by the National Academy of Sciences in 1916 to associate the broad community of science and technology with the Academy's purposes of furthering knowledge and advising the federal government. Functioning in accordance with general policies determined by the Academy, the Council has become the principal operating agency of both the National Academy of Sciences and the National Academy of Engineering in providing services to the government, the public, and the scientific and engineering communities. The Council is administered jointly by both Academies and the Institute of Medicine. Dr. Ralph J. Cicerone and Dr. Charles M. Vest are chair and vice chair, respectively, of the National Research Council.

www.national-academies.org

COMMITTEE ON COMMUNITY SUPERVISION
AND DESISTANCE FROM CRIME

JOAN PETERSILIA (*Cochair*), School of Social Ecology, University of California, Irvine
RICHARD ROSENFELD (*Cochair*), Department of Criminology and Criminal Justice, University of Missouri, St. Louis
RICHARD J. BONNIE, University of Virginia School of Law
ROBERT D. CRUTCHFIELD, Department of Sociology, University of Washington
MARK A.R. KLEIMAN, Department of Public Policy, University of California, Los Angeles
JOHN H. LAUB, Department of Criminology and Criminal Justice, University of Maryland
CHRISTY A. VISHER, Justice Policy Center, The Urban Institute, Washington, DC

CAROL PETRIE, *Study Director*
EUGENIA GROHMAN, *Senior Project Officer*
LINDA DePUGH, *Administrative Assistant*

COMMITTEE ON LAW AND JUSTICE
2006-2007

JAMES Q. WILSON *(Chair)*, Emeritus, University of California, Los Angeles
PHILIP J. COOK *(Vice Chair)*, Terry Sanford Institute of Public Policy, Duke University
DAVID H. BAYLEY, School of Criminal Justice, University of Albany, SUNY
RICHARD J. BONNIE, Institute of Law, Psychiatry, and Public Policy, University of Virginia Law School
MARTHA CRENSHAW, Department of Political Science, Wesleyan University
ROBERT D. CRUTCHFIELD, Department of Sociology, University of Washington
JOHN J. DIIULIO, JR., Institute of Government, University of Pennsylvania
STEVEN N. DURLAUF, Department of Economics, University of Wisconsin-Madison
JOHN A. FEREJOHN, Hoover Institution, Stanford University
ARTHUR S. GOLDBERGER, Department of Economics, University of Wisconsin-Madison
BRUCE HOFFMAN, Director, Washington Office, RAND Corporation
ROBERT L. JOHNSON, Chair of Pediatrics, UMDNJ-New Jersey Medical School
JOHN H. LAUB, Department of Criminology and Criminal Justice, University of Maryland
TRACEY L. MEARES, School of Law, University of Chicago
TERRIE E. MOFFITT, Institute of Psychiatry, University of London
MARK H. MOORE, Kennedy School of Government, Harvard University
RUTH PETERSON, Department of Sociology, Ohio State University
RICHARD ROSENFELD, Department of Criminology and Criminal Justice, University of Missouri-St. Louis
ROBERT J. SAMPSON, Department of Sociology, Harvard University
JEREMY TRAVIS, President, John Jay College of Criminal Justice, New York
CHRISTY VISHER, Justice Policy Center, The Urban Institute, Washington, DC

CAROL PETRIE, *Director*
BETTY CHEMERS, *Senior Program Officer*
LINDA DePUGH, *Program Associate*

COMMITTEE ON COMMUNITY SUPERVISION AND DESISTANCE FROM CRIME

JOAN PETERSILIA (*Cochair*), School of Social Ecology, University of California, Irvine
RICHARD ROSENFELD (*Cochair*), Department of Criminology and Criminal Justice, University of Missouri, St. Louis
RICHARD J. BONNIE, University of Virginia School of Law
ROBERT D. CRUTCHFIELD, Department of Sociology, University of Washington
MARK A.R. KLEIMAN, Department of Public Policy, University of California, Los Angeles
JOHN H. LAUB, Department of Criminology and Criminal Justice, University of Maryland
CHRISTY A. VISHER, Justice Policy Center, The Urban Institute, Washington, DC

CAROL PETRIE, *Study Director*
EUGENIA GROHMAN, *Senior Project Officer*
LINDA DePUGH, *Administrative Assistant*

COMMITTEE ON LAW AND JUSTICE
2006-2007

JAMES Q. WILSON *(Chair)*, Emeritus, University of California, Los Angeles
PHILIP J. COOK *(Vice Chair)*, Terry Sanford Institute of Public Policy, Duke University
DAVID H. BAYLEY, School of Criminal Justice, University of Albany, SUNY
RICHARD J. BONNIE, Institute of Law, Psychiatry, and Public Policy, University of Virginia Law School
MARTHA CRENSHAW, Department of Political Science, Wesleyan University
ROBERT D. CRUTCHFIELD, Department of Sociology, University of Washington
JOHN J. DIIULIO, JR., Institute of Government, University of Pennsylvania
STEVEN N. DURLAUF, Department of Economics, University of Wisconsin-Madison
JOHN A. FEREJOHN, Hoover Institution, Stanford University
ARTHUR S. GOLDBERGER, Department of Economics, University of Wisconsin-Madison
BRUCE HOFFMAN, Director, Washington Office, RAND Corporation
ROBERT L. JOHNSON, Chair of Pediatrics, UMDNJ-New Jersey Medical School
JOHN H. LAUB, Department of Criminology and Criminal Justice, University of Maryland
TRACEY L. MEARES, School of Law, University of Chicago
TERRIE E. MOFFITT, Institute of Psychiatry, University of London
MARK H. MOORE, Kennedy School of Government, Harvard University
RUTH PETERSON, Department of Sociology, Ohio State University
RICHARD ROSENFELD, Department of Criminology and Criminal Justice, University of Missouri-St. Louis
ROBERT J. SAMPSON, Department of Sociology, Harvard University
JEREMY TRAVIS, President, John Jay College of Criminal Justice, New York
CHRISTY VISHER, Justice Policy Center, The Urban Institute, Washington, DC

CAROL PETRIE, *Director*
BETTY CHEMERS, *Senior Program Officer*
LINDA DePUGH, *Program Associate*

Contents

Preface		ix
Executive Summary		1
1	Introduction and Background	7
2	Dimensions of Desistance	19
3	Parole: Current Practices	32
4	Services and Programs for Releasees	40
5	Criminal Justice Institutions and Community Resources	63
6	Conclusions, Recommendation, and Research Agenda	72
References		83
Appendixes		
A	Workshop Agenda	97
B	Biographical Sketches of Committee Members and Staff	100

Preface

Because the United States has the highest rate of imprisonment in the industrialized world, it also has the highest number of offenders—more than 600,000—returning to their communities, mostly cities, every year. Unfortunately, more than one-half of all released offenders will return to prison within 3 years of their release. The proportion of released offenders who return to prison has changed very little over the past three decades. It is in broad public interest to provide services and treatment in prison and as part of community supervision that will reduce the rate of recidivism—the return to prison for parole violations or the commission of new crimes. Reductions in recidivism would simultaneously reduce state corrections costs and improve community safety.

In this volume we attempt to pull together what is known from research about various models of community supervision designed to reduce recidivism and promote desistance from crime. We identify gaps in the research literature, and we discuss how currently available resources might best be used to improve community supervision outcomes.

This report is based in part on a workshop held by the Committee on Community Supervision and Desistance from Crime in January 2006. Four leading scholars presented papers to stimulate and guide the committee's discussion of traditional and new models of community supervision. The committee owes much to their work: David Farabee of the University of California Los Angeles; Faye S. Taxman of Virginia Commonwealth University; David B. Wexler, University of Arizona and University of Puerto

Rico; and Pamela K. Lattimore, University of South Carolina and Research Triangle Institute.

The committee's work was also aided by the workshop discussants, who represented a distinguished group from the research and practice communities: Michael Jacobson, Vera Institute in New York City; Martin Horn, commissioner, New York City Department of Corrections; Tom LeBel, University of Wisconsin, Milwaukee; Sharon Neumann, assistant deputy director, Community Sentencing Division, Oklahoma Department of Corrections; Jennifer L. Skeem, University of California, Irvine; Honorable Cindy Lederman, administrative judge, Eleventh Judicial Circuit, Juvenile Division, Miami-Dade County, Florida; Peggy B. Burke, Center for Effective Public Policy, Silver Spring, Maryland; and Jeremy Travis, president, John Jay College of Criminal Justice, New York City. The committee is grateful to all of these wonderful scholars and practitioners whose papers and comments provided such a sound foundation for this report.

The committee also offers grateful thanks to Glenn R. Schmitt, acting director of the National Institute of Justice (NIJ) at the time the workshop was held. He not only facilitated funding for the committee's work, but also gave unstintingly of his time and shared his ideas with the committee and workshop participants. The committee also thanks Thomas Feucht, assistant director for research and evaluation at NIJ for his invaluable support for this project, and Patrick Clark, acting director of the evaluation division at NIJ, who first broached the idea of focusing on desistance and the ways in which community supervision could foster less or zero offending among those released from prison.

The successful reintegration of former prisoners is one of the most formidable challenges facing society today. We hope that this volume will be of practical use to both the research and corrections communities in helping released offenders to desist from crime and become fully integrated and law-abiding citizens. This report has been reviewed in draft form by individuals chosen for their diverse perspectives and technical expertise, in accordance with procedures approved by the National Research Council's Report Review Committee. The purpose of this independent review is to provide candid and critical comments that will assist the institution in making its published report as sound as possible and to ensure that the report meets institutional standards for objectivity, evidence, and responsiveness to the study charge. The review comments and draft manuscript remain confidential to protect the integrity of the deliberative process.

We thank the following individuals for their review of this report: Shawn Bushway, Program on the Economics of Crime and Justice Policy, School of Criminal Justice, University at Albany, State University of New York; Michael E. Ezell, Department of Sociology, Vanderbilt University; Julie Horney, Office of the Dean, School of Criminal Justice, University at

Albany, State University of New York; Lila Kazemian, Department of Sociology, John Jay College of Criminal Justice/City University of New York; Michael D. Maltz, Criminal Justice and Information and Decision Sciences (emeritus), University of Illinois at Chicago; Ray Paternoster, Department of Criminology, University of Maryland, College Park; Alex R. Piquero, John Jay College of Criminal Justice/City University of New York; Steven Raphael, Richard and Rhoda Goldman School of Public Policy, University of California, Berkeley; and Amy L. Solomon, The Urban Institute, Washington, DC.

Although the reviewers listed above have provided many constructive comments and suggestions, they were not asked to endorse the conclusions or recommendations, nor did they see the final draft of the report before its release. The review of this report was overseen by Alfred Blumstein, The H. John Heinz III School of Public Policy and Management, Carnegie Mellon University. Appointed by the National Research Council, he was responsible for making certain that an independent examination of this report was carried out in accordance with institutional procedures and that all review comments were carefully considered. Responsibility for the final content of this report rests entirely with the authoring committee and the institution.

> Joan Petersilia and Richard Rosenfeld
> *Cochairs*, Committee on Community
>   Supervision and Desistance from Crime

Executive Summary

Every day, about 1,600 people are released from prisons in the United States. Of these 600,000 new releasees every year, about 480,000 are subject to parole or some other kind of postrelease supervision.

Prison releasees represent a challenge, both to themselves and to the communities to which they return. Will the releasees see parole as an opportunity to be reintegrated into society, with jobs and homes and supportive families and friends? Or will they commit new crimes or violate the terms of their parole contracts? If so, will they be returned to prison or placed under more stringent community supervision? Will the communities to which they return see them as people to be reintegrated or people to be avoided? And, the institution of parole itself is challenged with three different functions: to facilitate reintegration for parolees who are ready for rehabilitation; to deter crime; and to apprehend those parolees who commit new crimes and return them to prison.

In recent decades, policy makers, researchers, and program administrators have focused almost exclusively on "recidivism," which is essentially the failure of releasees to refrain from crime or stay out of prison. In contrast, for this study the National Institute of Justice (NIJ) of the U.S. Department of Justice asked the National Research Council to focus on "desistance," which broadly covers continued absence of criminal activity and requires reintegration into society. Specifically, the committee was asked (1) to consider the current state of parole practices, new and emerging models of community supervision, and what is necessary for successful reentry and (2) to provide a research agenda on the effects of community supervision on desistance from criminal activity, adherence to conditions of parole, and successful reentry into the community. To carry out its charge, the committee organized and held a workshop focused on traditional and new models of community supervision, the empirical underpinnings of such models, and the infrastructure necessary to support successful reentry. The committee also reviewed the literature on desistance from crime, community supervision, and the evaluation research on selected types of intervention.

FINDINGS

Parolees are a heterogeneous group, and their rates of desistance from crime vary widely: that is, there is no average parolee. Parolees who have short criminal records or have committed violent offenses have lower rates of recidivism than parolees who have long criminal records or have committed drug or property crimes. Releasees who have just served their first prison sentence have sharply lower rates of recidivism than those who have been imprisoned more than once, regardless of the sex, age, or race of the person or the type of crime. Among all parolees, many have significant education and cognitive deficits, as well as substance abuse and mental health problems.

Contrary to the commonly quoted conclusion that "nothing works," the evidence shows that some approaches work for some offenders and that other approaches show promise. Post release interventions that have shown measurable effects include treatment for substance abuse, especially when combined with frequent testing for drug abuse, and cognitive behavioral therapy. Comprehensive, multiservice employment and training programs and mentoring programs hold promise but require rigorous evaluation.

The committee offers a number of significant findings. First, cognitive-behavioral treatment programs reduce recidivism significantly. Second, the peak rates of committing a new crime or violating the terms of parole occur in the first days, weeks, and months after release. Third, deaths among releasees are very high in the first weeks after release, more than 12 times the average for the general population. Clearly, the first days and weeks out of prison are the riskiest for both releasees and the general public.

In addition, extensive longitudinal research on desistance highlights specific conditions that lead to less offending: good and stable marriages and strong ties to work appear to be particularly important. These findings seem somewhat at odds with findings from program evaluation that individual-level change, including shifts in cognitive thinking, education, and drug treatment, are likely to be more effective than programs that increase opportunities for work, reunite families, and provide housing. We caution, however, that many findings on the effects of desistance programs are limited, generally because of inadequate program implementation and because of failure to fully account for self-selection bias in evaluations.

These findings have major implications for the design of services and interventions, for both parole systems and other community-based programs. A first-time parolee who committed a violent crime needs a different program than a drug-using repeat parolee who committed a drug crime. However, concentrating supervision and services in the first days and weeks out of prison is likely to have most effects on desistance.

RECOMMENDATIONS

The evidence on the rates of death and crime commission within the first weeks of a person's release argue strongly for a redirection of postrelease program and service provision efforts to those first days and weeks after release. We recommend that parole authorities and administrators of both in-prison and postrelease programs redesign their activities and redirect their resources to provide major support to parolees and other releasees at the time of release. Such programs may take many different forms, including: intensive and detailed prerelease and postrelease counseling; immediate enrollment in drug treatment programs, intense parole supervision; assistance in finding work; short-term halfway houses; mentors who are available at the moment of release; and assistance in obtaining identification, clothes, and other immediate needs. The key is that a person should not leave prison without an immediately available person and plan for postrelease life.

We also recommend that longer term assistance for parolees include cognitive-behavioral treatment approaches.

RESEARCH NEEDS

Future research on parole and desistance needs to be more methodologically rigorous. In program design, random assignment should be used when possible; when it is not possible, more attention is needed to the selection of comparison groups and to the use of appropriate statistical techniques to account for differences between program participants and comparison groups. In program implementation, more attention is needed to ensure fidelity to program principles and procedures. In program evaluation, more attention is needed to avoid the possibility of self-selection bias.

Rigorous research is needed to explain gaps between the research findings on what influences desistance and evaluation findings of program effects. Also needed are improvements in the conceptualization and design of program content based on research findings on desistance. Research is needed on how cognitive-behavioral treatment approaches can be expanded effectively to meet current demands.

The committee's findings and recommendation regarding the need for interventions at the point of release present a unique opportunity for research. Because different jurisdictions are likely to implement different programs for new releasees, these "natural experiments" can be systematically studied to learn what works best for which kinds of releasees. Closely related to research on early interventions for releasees is the question of whether people who are going to "fail" usually do so quickly or whether early interventions can make a difference—not only by delaying recidivism, but also by reducing it. A related question is whether the higher recidivism rate for offenders with multiple imprisonments is a function of their characteristics or the effects of the prison and postprison experiences.

There has been little research on the effects of parolees (and other releasees) on the local communities to which they return, particularly on crime rates. Also largely missing has been research on the validity and significance of the arrest data for parolees. For example, do parolees actually commit more crimes than people with similar characteristics who live in the same neighborhoods, or are parolees arrested more often only because they are under closer scrutiny? There is a related question from the reverse perspective. What are the effects of neighborhood or community conditions—such as the presence of high crime rates or drug markets or the availability of social and treatment services—on parolees? A second related question is the role of arrests and returns to prison for violations of specific conditions of parole contracts, rather than for new crimes: Is imprisonment—rather than a short-term stay in jail or other sanction in the context of continued parole supervision—the best way to deal with such violations, particularly in light of the general overcrowding of U.S. prisons? Similarly, is the revocation of parole, rather than a new prosecution, the best way to deal with a new offense by a parolee?

Looking at the parole system itself, there has been little research on its effects. A range of questions need to be answered, including: What kinds of supervision work best with what kinds of releasees? What are the effects of policies that bar parolees from public-subsidized housing and other social services? Should parolees be released to places other than their home communities—particularly if such communities are high-crime areas—in order to promote desistance? How can technological approaches, such as the use of global positioning systems (GPSs), help parole authorities and promote desistance? How effective are incentives that reward and promote desistance (e.g., less intrusive supervision or the remission of fines), compared with relying solely on punishments for violating the terms of parole? What types of incentives are most effective both for increasing desistance

EXECUTIVE SUMMARY

among parolees and for increasing the performance and job satisfaction of parole officers?

The large number of parolees and other released prisoners in the country makes it urgent to carry out research on the conditions, policies, and programs that will promote desistance and successful reintegration into U.S. society.

1

Introduction and Background

On December 31, 2005, the latest date for which figures are available, the United States had a total incarceration rate of 737 per each 100,000 residents, by far the highest in the industrialized world. About two-thirds of the incarcerated population (491 persons per 100,000 population) were in federal and state prisons; the remainder were in local jails (Harrison and Beck, 2006). This rate reflects 30 years of steady growth in the use of imprisonment as punishment for both violent and nonviolent crimes. Because of the upsurge in imprisonment rates—a more than four-fold increase since 1980—the number of released prisoners has grown sharply during the past decade. Unprecedented numbers of individuals now live in U.S. communities under the supervision of parole, along with other former prisoners who are not under formal supervision.

Many parolees subsequently return to custody, creating a constant supply of offenders to feed ever-growing incarceration rates. These parolees and other former prisoners are the subject of this report. Appropriate strategies to interrupt this cycle and to manage parolees and other former prisoners are needed both to improve their chances for desistance from crime and reintegration in communities, and to protect public safety. These strategies must be based on the recognition that resources to help these populations are limited.

CONTEXT

The Population of Parolees

Roughly 600,000 people are released each year from state and federal prisons in the United States, about 1,600 a day.[1] Of the total, about 20 percent leave prison without any post-prison supervision requirement, usually because they have served their full sentence ("maxed out"). Of the 80 percent of offenders who leave prison before the end of their sentence, about 50 percent were released by mandate, and about 30 percent were released after review by a discretionary parole board. However, whether an inmate is released as a result of a mandatory or discretionary process, parole release is "conditional": parolees are to serve out the remainder of their sentences in the community under the supervision of state parole authorities.

All states except Maine and Virginia have mandatory or discretionary parole supervision (for releasees who have not maxed out), although some states have changed its name to distance themselves from negative associations with the term. The states' parolee population grew 247 percent from 1980 to 2004, from 220,400 to 765,350.[2] In 2004, 466,000 released prisoners entered state parole systems across the country. About 88 percent of the parolees were males; for both males and females, 40 percent were white, 41 percent were black, 18 percent were Hispanic, and the remaining 1 percent were non-Hispanics of other races. The average parolee in 2004 was in his or her mid-30s. About 38 percent had been convicted and imprisoned for a drug offense, 26 percent for a property offense, and 24 percent for a violent offense. The remaining 12 percent had been imprisoned for other crimes, primarily public order offenses. The average time served in prison in 2002, the latest date for which statistics are available, was 29 months (median time served was 17 months) (Bureau of Justice Statistics, 2002). Eventually, 93 percent of all U.S. prisoners will be released (Petersilia, 2003).

The Parole and Reentry Systems

As long as there have been prisons, societies have struggled with how best to help prisoners reintegrate in society when they are released.[3] In the

---

[1] Unless indicated otherwise, the statistics cited in this section are from the Bureau of Justice Statistics (BJS): http://www.ojp.usdoj.gov/bjs [September 2006].

[2] An additional 86,567 parolees were under federal jurisdiction in 2004. Parole under the federal system has been periodically abolished, altered, and reinstated over the years; for the history of the U. S. Parole Commission, see http://www.usdoj.gov/uspc/history.htm [October 2006].

[3] This section is drawn from Petersilia (2003).

United States, prisoners who have not maxed out are released to parole supervision. Whether they are released through a discretionary or mandatory process, the majority of released prisoners will be subject to some sort of post-prison or parole supervision.[4] Parole is the responsibility of the executive branch of government. In most states, it is administered by a board or commission appointed by the governor.

Parole, common in the United States for at least a century, can legally be defined as releasing offenders from a correctional institution, after they have served a portion of their sentence, under the continued custody of the state and under conditions that permit their reincarceration in the event of a violation of the terms of parole (which may otherwise not be a criminal offense). Parole, unlike probation, always occurs after some part of a court-imposed prison term has been completed.

No prisoner has a legal right to parole. Rather, it is a privilege a state grants, through a contractual arrangement with a prisoner, who signs a parole release contract in exchange for the promise to abide by specified conditions. A state authority retains legal control of parolees until they are formally dismissed from parole, which usually lasts between 1 to 3 years.[5]

Parole agents (or officers) are responsible for ensuring that parolees fulfill the terms of their contracts. Most agents have the legal authority to carry and use firearms and to search places, persons, and property without a warrant and without probable cause (otherwise required by the Fourth Amendment to the U.S. Constitution). The search power applies to the household where a parolee is living and the business place where a parolee is working. The ability to arrest, confine, and, in some cases re-imprison a parolee for violating the conditions of the parole agreement gives parole agents a great deal of discretionary authority.

Parole conditions can be roughly classified as general, applicable to all parolees, and tailored, applicable to particular offenders. Standard parole conditions are similar throughout most jurisdictions and usually include not committing crimes, not carrying a weapon, seeking and maintaining employment, reporting changes of address, reporting to one's parole agent, and paying required victim and court restitution costs.

Tailored conditions are reserved for certain kinds of offenders or crimes.

---

[4]In indeterminate sentencing systems, a parole board releases inmates to parole supervision on the basis of statutory or administrative determinations of eligibility. Inmates usually must serve some fraction of the minimum or maximum sentence before becoming eligible for parole. In determinate sentencing systems, inmates are conditionally released from prison when they have served their original sentence minus time off for good behavior.

[5]Parole supervision can last much longer in some states: for example, Texas parole supervision is often for 10 to 20 years. A number of recently enacted laws require life-time supervision and registration of sex offenders.

Tailored conditions for sex offenders may require parolees to participate in sex offender therapy, register as sex offenders, and refrain from entering child safety zones. People convicted of domestic assaults may be required not to contact their spouses, domestic partners, or other injured or threatened family members. A growing number of parolees are now required to register with the police when released from prison. Originally begun for sex offenders, registration is now required of parolees convicted of arson, crimes against children, domestic violence, stalking, and other offenses. The most common special condition for parolees is drug testing.

Some criminal justice experts argue that few parolees can meet all of the more stringent conditions and that imposing and enforcing them almost guarantees failure. But many state legislatures have become more "anticrime" in recent years, which has translated into both stricter requirements for granting parole and stricter supervision and easier revocation procedures for parolees.

If a parolee commits a new crime or fails to meet the conditions of the parole contract, parole can be revoked and the parolee can be returned to prison. Violations of parole conditions are often termed "technical violations," but this characterization can be misleading because the conditions encompass important obligations, such as refraining from contacting a previous victim or from using alcohol, as well as purely procedural requirements, such as checking in with the parole officer. Because parolees are still in the formal legal custody of prison authorities, their constitutional rights are severely limited. When parole agents identify a violation by a parolee, they notify their supervisors, who can initiate procedures to return a parolee to prison.

High parole revocation rates are one of the major factors linked to the growing U.S. prison population. Each year, about 300,000 parolees are sent back to prison. About 70 percent of returned prisoners self-report that their parole was revoked because of an arrest or conviction for a new offense; 22 percent said they had absconded or otherwise failed to report to a parole officer; 16 percent said they had a drug-related violation; and 18 percent reported other reasons, such as failure to maintain employment or to meet financial obligations (Hughes et al., 2001). Some prisoners are returned for two or more reasons. The number of offenders who are reincarcerated due to parole revocation increased more than sevenfold between 1980 and 1999; 42 percent of the growth in total admissions to state prisons during that period was the result of revocations for violations of specified parole conditions (Blumstein and Beck, 2005).

Parolees are required to report to their designated parole field office within a few days of release. In most states, parolees are legally required to return to the county of their last residence. The vast majority of parolees—80 percent—are supervised on "regular" caseloads, averaging 67 cases to one parole officer, in which they are seen (face to face) less than twice a month (Petersilia, 1999). Officers also may contact family members or employers to inquire about the parolee's progress.

Parole agents, in addition to monitoring contract compliance, also provide counseling and broker community resources. In fact, parole agents historically have played an important role in providing job assistance, family counseling, and chemical dependency testing and treatment programs, mixing authority with help. This mixture is now sometimes seen as a conflict—service versus surveillance. In a way, parole officers can be thought of as gun-carrying social workers. Today, parole agents seldom provide direct counseling services, but many do still orchestrate referrals to community agencies. Of course, the help parolees receive differs vastly, depending on the state and jurisdiction in which they are being supervised.

In addition to regular caseloads, most parole agencies also have specialized caseloads designed to provide group counseling for such conditions as drug use and unemployment or for the special concerns raised by the supervision of mentally ill people, people with developmental disabilities, and sex offenders. However, this is a very small part of most parole systems: overall, less than 4 percent of all parolees are supervised on specialized caseloads (Petersilia, 2003). Virtually every state uses a classification system for assigning parolees to different levels of supervision and specialized caseloads.

Many parole officers are frustrated because they lack the time and resources to do the kind of job they believe is maximally helpful to their clients. Parole officers often complain that paperwork has increased, their clients have more serious problems, and that their caseloads are much higher than the 35-50 cases that have been considered the ideal caseload for a parole officer. As Michael Jacobson (2005, p. 155) recently wrote:

> Parole officers are doing exactly what parole systems ask them to do; they work with few resources and experience constant pressure, including anxieties about whether someone on their caseload will be the next murderer of a Polly Klass. Indeed, a combination of high caseloads, few internal resources, and frequently, political condemnation makes their job one of the most difficult and stressful in the criminal justice system.

One naturally wonders whether simply reducing an officer's caseload would result in more compliance with parole contracts and fewer new criminal offenses. A national demonstration project that evaluated the effects of reduced caseloads actually showed higher rates of violations of parole agreements for parolees who were supervised on small caseloads, because officers were able to watch them more closely to uncover more of their misdeeds (Petersilia and Turner, 1993). But this study also found that when probationers and parolees were subject to *both* surveillance and appropriate treatment, their arrest rates were 10 to 20 percent lower than other probationers and parolees. Program evaluations in Texas, Wisconsin, Oregon, and Colorado have shown similarly encouraging results.

High-quality parole supervision costs more than regular supervision, and the program costs are driven by the risks and needs of participants and the surveillance and services provided. Currently, about $2,000-$4,000 per year per parolee is spent for regular parole supervision. The average yearly cost of supervising the 117,000 parolees in California (18 percent of all U.S. state parolees are in California) is now $4,067 per parolee, while parole failures cost the state $10,000 per parolee (California Legislative Analyst's Office, 2004). In contrast, other intermediate sanctions—such as electronic monitoring, day reporting centers, or effective substance abuse programs—are estimated to cost between $5,000 and $20,000 per client per year.

Public Policy Issues

Parolees pose multiple challenges for the communities to which they are released. Many leave prison with unresolved substance abuse and mental health problems, lack of skills for employment, and have housing needs. A majority (53%) of state inmates used illicit drugs in the month before their offense, while a third (32%) committed their current offense under the influence of drugs. Nearly one-half of the violent offenders in state prisons (47%) met the criteria for recent drug dependence or abuse, and 10 percent said the need to get money for drugs was a motive in their crimes (Mumola and Karberg, 2006). Participation in drug abuse programs has increased among state and federal inmates with recent drug use histories, but it is still surprisingly low. Among state inmates who used drugs in the month before the offense, only 39 percent reported taking part in drug treatment or other drug programs since admission (Mumola and Karberg, 2006).

The deinstitutionalization policy that started in the 1960s shifted the focus of care of people with mental illness from psychiatric hospitals to local communities. As a result, states closed many of their mental hospitals and people with mental illnesses were increasingly arrested and jailed; most of them are eventually released on parole. In a BJS study of mental illness, using prisoners' self-reports, Ditton (1999) reported that 16.2 percent of state prison inmates were estimated to be mentally ill, reporting either a mental or emotional condition or an overnight stay in a mental hospital or program. Among parolees, 12 percent were homeless at the time of their arrest, and they face significant housing barriers at release (see Petersilia, 2003).

If parolees commit a new criminal offense or violate the specified conditions of parole supervision (e.g., fail a drug test), they can be returned to prison to serve out the remainder of the sentence for which they were originally convicted and incarcerated or to serve a new sentence. Regardless of how it is measured, the "failure" rate is very high among released prisoners. A BJS study of state prisoners released in 15 states in 1994 found that fully two-thirds were rearrested and just over one-half were returned to prison within 3 years (Langan and Levin, 2002). The probability of rearrest was higher among males, younger people, property offenders, and those with longer arrest records. Rearrest prevalence also was significantly higher among parolees who had previously been incarcerated and released than among first-time parolees, even with age, offense type, prior arrests, and other predictors controlled (Rosenfeld et al., 2005). This population of "repeat parolees" poses especially difficult challenges to parole agencies, if only because they have failed at community reentry at least once before.

In the BJS study, rearrest rates among parolees released in 1994 were sharply higher during the next 3 years than arrest rates in the general population. Parolees accounted for an estimated 10-15 percent of all violent, property, and drug arrests between 1994 and 1997, and the share of total arrests attributable to released prisoners grew as general crime rates declined during the 1990s (Rosenfeld et al., 2005). Most released prisoners who are arrested for new crimes will be returned to prison—and most of them will be released again.

The strain on communities to deal with released prisoners has increased in recent years as a result of several factors. More people are being sentenced to terms of incarceration and, consequently, the number being released on parole at any given time has grown. In addition, many prisoners are transferred from one institution to another for disciplinary purposes or to relieve crowding, leaving less time for longer term programs that might help offenders prepare for release and reintegration in society. There has also been less money (on a per person basis) for such programs in recent years. Prerelease programs are not flexible enough to set priorities for services on the basis of the distribution of time served in the population needing programs. The increase in mandatory supervised parole also has led to larger caseloads for parole agents. Here, too, in most states, there have not been increases in funds for parole supervision commensurate with the increase in the number of parolees.

TERMINOLOGY

Many terms are used to characterize both people currently in jail or prison and those who have spent time in those institutions. For clarity and to frame the discussion, we have adopted the terminology laid out in this section. We note first that although the focus of this report is almost exclusively on people who have been released from prisons, some of the terms and some of the discussion also include people released from jails.[6]

The terms "inmate" and "incarcerated" refer to people in prison (or jail). People who have been released from a prison or jail after serving a sentence are "releasees." This term covers everyone who has spent time in a prison (or jail): people who served their full terms; people who served less than their full terms because of time off for good behavior, prison crowding, or any other reason; people with a formal parole agreement; and people under any other kind of post-incarceration supervision. The term excludes people who left jails without being charged or were exonerated at trial. It also excludes people on probation—those who have been found guilty but not sent to jail or prison—and those whose final sentencing will depend on their behavior while on probation.

The term "parolee" is used to refer to persons who are currently on parole, under the supervision of parole authorities, whether released by a parole board or some other mechanism. Where the term releasee is used interchangeably with parolee it should be understood to mean releasee's minus those who have served their full term.

"Reentry" is the process of leaving prison and returning to a community. "Reintegration" is the most recently used term to define the transition from incarceration to life outside an institution, in a community. However, in this report, reentry is used interchangeably with reintegration. Reentry is a more neutral term: reentry can be successful or not, and there is a continuum. One can think of completely successful reentry as a person's having a place to live, a job, not committing crimes, and otherwise being a fully integrated member of a community. At the other end of the continuum, one can think of homelessness, unemployment, and the violation of the terms of parole or the commission of new crimes as characteristic of failed reentry. Successful reentry may facilitate the maintenance of desistance from crime. Desistance is a term that shifts the focus of policy from the negative to the positive: instead of focusing on the releasees who return to prison, it focuses on those who refrain from or lessen their criminal behavior as well as other negative behaviors, such as substance abuse, that may lead to crime or violations of specified conditions of release.

Although "recidivism" is a common term in criminal justice, we try to use it as little possible in this report, for four reasons. First, it covers people returned to prison both for violating the terms of parole and for committing new criminal offenses, yet for public policy purposes it may be useful

---

[6]Generally speaking, prisons are run by states or the federal government and house people sentenced to terms of more than 1 year; jails are run by counties or other local jurisdictions and house people who have been arrested but not yet charged, who have been charged but not yet tried, or who are serving sentences of less than 1 year.

to consider these two populations separately. Second, the term focuses on the negative outcome for releasees: again, for public policy purposes, it may be more useful to focus on what programs or interventions can contribute to a positive outcome. Third, the term implies a simple 0 or 1 outcome: either a person is returned to prison or not; yet desistance from criminal behavior, like cessation of smoking or drug use or even dieting, may involve several attempts over time. If some people desist from committing offenses for longer and longer periods of time or otherwise moderate their criminal behavior, it is useful information for policy makers. Finally, our charge (see below) does not use the term. However, given that much of the research in criminal justice uses the term and attempts to measure recidivism, we cannot completely eliminate the word from our analyses or our report.

An underlying public policy issue that is related to terminology is the goal of parole as a crime control method: Is the goal to send noncompliant parolees back to prison as quickly as possible or to facilitate desistance from criminal behavior? This basic question affects how policy makers, as well as police, parole agents, and others in the criminal justice system, view their jobs and the parolees.

COMMITTEE CHARGE AND APPROACH

The National Institute of Justice (NIJ) of the U.S. Department of Justice asked the National Research Council to establish an ad hoc committee to conduct a workshop-based study on the role of parole and other forms of postrelease supervision in promoting the rehabilitation and successful reentry of former prisoners, including their desistance from criminal activity and their reintegration into families, neighborhoods, the workforce, and the civic life of the community.

In accordance with the terms of the charge, the workshop focused on the empirical underpinnings and evaluations of new or emerging models of community supervision and the likelihood that these kinds of models can promote various distinct outcomes, such as desistance from crime and adherence to conditions of parole, as well as institutional support for the service needs of ex-prisoners and their families. The workshop provided a basis for the development of a research agenda that is addressed in the report.

The presentations and discussions at the workshop were designed to consider the following topics:

1. Data and research on traditional and current parole practices in order to understand the current state of practice in parole and other forms of post release supervision.

2. New and emerging models of community supervision, especially the empirical or theoretical underpinnings or evaluations of these models and their effect on desistance as well as on successful reentry.
3. The infrastructures necessary for successful reentry and the role of community supervision in those infrastructures.
4. A research agenda on the effects of community supervision on different outcomes, such as desistance from further criminal activity; adherence to conditions of parole and successful reentry into the community.

The request from NIJ reflects both public concern and congressional attention. In 2005, legislation was introduced in both houses of Congress calling for both new grants and the continuation of existing programs to encourage successful prisoner reentry. The proposed legislation also called for studies of the effects on children of having an incarcerated parent; the characteristics and circumstances of former prisoners who do not return to prison; and returning prisoners who present special challenges, such as having severe mental illness, and those who represent the greatest threat to public safety. Although this legislative proposal was not enacted, it is clear that the subject of the reentry of former prisoners to society is a major public policy issue.

In looking at releasees, it is important to recognize that prisoners reentering society are a small proportion—less than 10 percent—of the approximately 7 million people who are under supervision of the criminal justice system at any given time. The total includes people awaiting trial, people on probation and parole, and people in jails and prison (Bureau of Justice Statistics, 2006b). By far the largest group is people on probation, who in 2004 accounted for almost 60 percent of the total (Bureau of Justice Statistics, 2006a).

Although parolees make up a relatively small percentage of people under supervision of the criminal justice system, the total, as noted above, is now more than 600,000 annually. Moreover, most of the people released from prisons go to a small number of cities—about 20—and to neighborhoods in those cities that have some of the highest crime rates in the nation (Travis, 2005). Because parolees who have been released more than once before have very high reoffending rates their effect on these communities can be significant, and what can be done to support their successful reentry to society is therefore critical to neighborhood stability. Although this report focuses only on people released from prisons and under parole supervision in the community, some of the issues may well be the same for other people who reside in these high-crime communities, particularly probationers.

The Committee on Community Supervision and Desistance from Crime held its workshop on January 18, 2006, in Irvine, California. Papers were presented by four distinguished researchers, and there were two discussants for each paper, one researcher, and one practitioner (see Appendix A for the workshop agenda). The four topics of the presentations and discussion had been selected by the committee as possibly important issues in carrying out its charge: (1) Is treatment the road to rehabilitation? Promoting offender change through accountability; (2) a behavioral management approach to supervision; (3) searching for a judicial model of reentry and community supervision; and (4) triage: resource allocation for probation and parole. After the workshop, the committee commissioned a fifth paper on faith-based programs for ex-offenders.

The committee met twice in the months following the workshop, to consider the topics discussed at the workshop, the issue of faith-based programs, and what turned out to be significant new research on important aspects of desistance and community supervision. The committee did not complete its work as quickly as it had anticipated, in large part because of the new work we identified and the need to integrate those findings with older work. While there is still a great deal that is not known about the processes of desistance and community supervision of former prisoners, the committee is encouraged that research is identifying some effective policies and practices, as well as key questions for future research.

SCOPE OF THE REPORT

After its workshop, the committee held two meetings to consider revised versions of the papers and develop this report, based on the papers and the broader literature in the field. Because of the limits on our resources, we have had to be highly selective with respect to the specific populations, issues, and topics covered in this report. As indicated above, our focus is on parolees—people released from prison and supervised in the community. We do not address the distinctive issues associated with the supervision and desistance from crime of the much larger population of probationers: people who are sentenced to community supervision in lieu of imprisonment. Nor do we address the problems and needs of people who are awaiting trial or are serving sentences of 1 year or less in local jails.

There are also several classes of offenders that we do not consider explicitly, in part because of the lack of research. We do not explicitly consider the special legal, supervision, and treatment issues connected with sex offenders, a topic of great public concern and controversy that merits its own comprehensive assessment. We note, however, that more than 95 percent of parolees are not sex offenders. We also do not separately consider juveniles, who are generally believed to have distinct problems and needs.

Many of the needs, challenges, and treatment and supervision considerations that apply to parolees also apply to other populations of ex-offenders; in fact, most parolees at one time or another also serve probation sentences and spend time in local jails. It is best, then, to think of a parolee not as a special kind of *person*, but as a distinctive criminal justice *status* with similarities to and differences from other statuses. We identify these similarities and differences as appropriate throughout the report.

Chapter 2 of the report looks at concepts and definitions of desistance, which are critical to understanding how parole works and how it might work differently. Chapter 3 then examines how parole currently works. Chapter 4 looks at the services and programs that are available for parolees (and, in most cases, other releasees) and the evidence about their effectiveness. Chapter 5 considers community issues—what burdens do parolees place on them and what can they offer to parolees—with particular attention to courts. Chapter 6 presents the committee's summary of what is known and what needs to be known about parole and desistance, including reintegration of former prisoners.

Our treatment of each of these topics is guided by the report's overarching themes of the *heterogeneity* of the parole population and intervention effects, especially the *implementation challenges* of policies and programs designed to improve the supervision of parolees in communities, address their service and treatment needs, and facilitate desistance from reoffending.

Our analysis is constrained by the paucity of research that has been done and its limitations. The most prominent limitation—in terms of this report—is the lack of specificity about the population of study: parolees and other releasees are rarely distinguished in the research. Another limitation is the lack of comprehensive jurisdiction- and individual-level data on the characteristics of parolees and their prison and post-prison experiences. We address these and other research limitations in the report's final chapter.

2

Dimensions of Desistance

CONCEPT AND DEFINITIONS

Zero Offending or Less Offending?

"Desistance" from crime is a common term in criminal justice research.[1] Most offenders, after all, eventually stop offending. Yet there is relatively little theoretical conceptualization about crime cessation, the various reasons for desistance, or the mechanisms underlying it.

Conceptually, there are several fundamental questions about desistance. For example, can desistance occur after one act of crime? If so, are the processes of desistance from a single act of crime different from those following several acts of crime? Is there such a thing as "spontaneous remission"? If so, can the term be precisely defined? One definition of spontaneous remission is desistance that occurs absent any external intervention (Stall and Biernacki, 1986). How can permanent desistance (the absence of acts of crime forever) be distinguished from temporary desistance (the absence of crimes for some amount of time)?

Should a change from serious criminal acts to less serious ones be characterized as a type of desistance? In a similar vein, if criminal acts cease, but other problem behaviors (such as alcoholism or other drug use) persist or increase, what does it mean about the nature of desistance? All of these

---

[1]This section is drawn from Laub and Sampson (2001)

issues raise critical questions about the meaning of desistance, and, consequently, about how to measure it or determine whether it is occurring.

Whether using official records or self-reports, it is clear that how one defines desistance affects the measures and determinations about who desists and the relative size of the desisting population (for discussion of these issues, respectively, see Bushway et al., 2003; Brame et al., 2003). Kazemian (2007) reviews various operational definitions in past studies of desistance, which include convictions at age 21 but not between ages 21 and 32 (Farrington and Hawkins, 1991), the absence of a new officially recorded offense or probation violation in a 2-year period (Kruttschnitt et al., 2000) and the absence of self-reported illegal earnings during a 1-year period (Pezzin, 1995; see also Kazemian, 2007: Table 1, for more details from additional studies). Kazemian (2007, p. 8) concludes that the "substantial degree of variability in the conceptualization of desistance . . . has led to disparate results regarding the causes and correlates of desistance from crime."

The issue of reintegration in society is considered as part of desistance in this report because the committee believes it may be a necessary condition for the maintenance of desistance. A recent National Research Council (2005) report notes that there is little standardization of how outcomes such as desistance or recidivism should be measured in the evaluation of programs. Moreover, the findings on desistance from crime as a result of informal social controls come from longitudinal research, not program evaluation research. Empirical work is needed to examine how different definitions of desistance, as well as different research approaches, affect research outcomes.

There is currently no agreed-on definition of desistance, but there is a growing consensus among researchers that it is best defined as a process, not an event, in which the frequency of crimes decelerates and exhibits less variety (see Bushway et al., 2001; Laub and Sampson, 2003; Maruna, 2001; Uggen and Massoglia, 2003; Weitekamp and Kerner, 1994; Loeber and LeBlanc, 1990; LeBlanc and Fréchette, 1989). For example, Maruna (2001, p. 17) defines desistance not as an event that happens, but, rather, as "the sustained absence of a certain type of event (in this case, crime)."

A National Research Council report (1986) noted that care must be taken not to erroneously attribute the absence of further crime events near the end of an observation period or at the end of a specific age to (career) desistance rather than to the random time between events. Improved measures of the permanent absence of offending, which remains the clearest definition of desistance from crime, are needed.

Laub and Sampson (2001, 2003) have argued that it is important to analytically distinguish termination of offending from the concept of desistance: "termination" refers to the time at which one stops criminal activity, while "desistance" is the causal process that supports the termination of offending. While it is difficult to ascertain when the process of desistance actually begins, it is apparent that it continues after the termination of offending. In their view, the process of desistance maintains the continued state of nonoffending.

More Prosocial Outcomes

In addition to the cessation or reduction of criminal activities, the concept of desistance as a process generally also encompasses positive outcomes in terms of individuals' behavior and integration into society. "[The] successful establishment of bonds with conventional others and participation in conventional activities are major contingencies on the path that leads to termination of a criminal career" (Shover, 1996, p. 126). More recently, Uggen and Massoglia (2003, p. 317) have argued that "desistance is a process characterized by particular behavioral states or markers" that is marked by the assumption of "adult occupational and family roles" (2003, p. 317). Along similar lines, Maruna (2001, p. 7) has contended that desistance is only possible when ex-offenders "develop a coherent, prosocial identity for themselves." Thus, desistance is also generally viewed in terms of social integration or reintegration.

Marriage

Family and work seem to be especially important in the desistance process. The association of marriage with lower crime among men has been widely reported in both quantitative and qualitative studies (Farrington and West, 1995; Horney et al., 1995; Irwin, 1970; Laub and Sampson, 2003; Maume et al., 2005; Sampson and Laub, 1993; Shover, 1996; Warr, 1998; for a general overview, see Laub and Sampson, 2001). Marriage, especially strong marital attachment, has thus been identified as a significant factor in desistance for men.

Recent research has extended this finding to women (King et al., 2007), but the researchers find the effects for marriage are less robust for women than they are for men. The King et al. study is an important one because it uses propensity score matching to estimate the causal effects of marriage. They use a contemporary dataset (The National Youth Survey), and they extend the analysis of marriage and crime to men and women. They find marriage reduces offending for males, especially for those men with a low propensity to marry. They find that marriage reduces offending for females, but only for those with a moderate propensity to marry.

A change in criminal behavior may not necessarily result from marriage alone; rather, a change may occur in response to an enduring attachment that emerges from entering into a good marriage. From this perspective, the growth of social bonds is like an investment process (Laub and Sampson, 1993, pp. 310-311; Nagin and Paternoster, 1994, pp. 586-588). As the investment in social bonds grows, the incentive for avoiding crime increases because more is at stake. Empirical support for the idea of marriage as an investment process comes from research findings that early marriages characterized by social cohesiveness led to a growing preventive effect (Laub et al., 1998).

Marriage also influences desistance because it often leads to significant changes in everyday routines. It is well known that life-styles and routine activities are a major source of variation in exposure to crime and victimization (Hindelang et al., 1978; Cohen and Felson, 1979). For example, participation in unstructured socializing activities with peers increases the frequency of deviant behaviors among those ages 18 to 26 (Osgood et al., 1996). Marriage has the potential to radically alter routine activities, especially with regard to one's peer group. As Osgood and Lee (1993) have argued, marriage entails obligations that tend to reduce leisure activities outside of the family. It is reasonable to assume that married people will spend more time together than with their same-sex peers. There is supporting empirical evidence that the transition to marriage is followed by a decline in time spent with friends and with exposure to delinquent peers (Warr, 1998, p. 183). Marriage, therefore, has the potential to cut off an ex-offender from peers at risk of re-offending.

A recent study has addressed the issue of the causal direction of the relationship between marriage and desistance from crime. That study (Sampson et al., 2006) adopted a counterfactual life-course approach using yearly data from a sample of a group of 500 high-risk boys followed prospectively from adolescence to age 32 and a subsample of 52 men followed to age 70. The researchers found that being married is associated with an average reduction of approximately 35 percent in the odds of a criminal act for the married men in comparison with the nonmarried men (see also King et al., 2007).

The researchers argue that marriage has a "knifing off" effect in the lives of disadvantaged men. They theorize that marriage may offer the opportunity for new relationships and social supports; may change the routine activities engaged in by these men, especially unstructured time with peers; may create a more structured set of activities that are in many ways "supervised" by the spouse; and may transform the identity of the offender in ways that allow a life of greater responsibility as a spouse and parent (Laub and Sampson, 2003).

While these results are robust, supporting the inference that states of marriage causally inhibit crime over a person's life, the data used in the study are not recent. Using more recent data from the 1970s, Piquero and his colleagues (2002) found that conventional marriages inhibited continuity in criminal activity generally for both whites and nonwhites. However, the researchers found that conventional marriage did not appear to significantly inhibit violent arrests among nonwhites. They also found that common-law marriages increased crime (both violent and nonviolent) for nonwhites, but was insignificant for whites.

Using data based on interviews with 658 newly convicted male offenders sentenced to the Nebraska Department of Correctional Services during a 9-month period in 1989-1990, Horney et al. (1995) also found that while marriage reduces offending, cohabitation increases it (Horney et al., 1995, p. 659). This finding is important in light of the fact that by 2002, only 48 percent of black families were headed by married couples, down from 70 percent during the 1960s (Kinnon, 2003; Wilson, 2002), and that one factor influencing this decline is the rise of incarceration rates, among black men since 1980 (Cready, Fossett, and Kiecolt, 1997). It would be important, therefore, to study the effects of marriage on reentry outcomes among a contemporary population of released prisoners. Data on the effects of marriage on this reentering population are needed.

Building on research about the positive effects of healthy marriages, the Administration for Children, Youth and Families (ACF) in the U.S. Department of Health and Human Services (DHHS) has designed and funded the Community Healthy Marriage Initiative (CHMI), a nationwide program that has been implemented in over 20 sites (U.S. Department of Health and Human Services, 2007). A national evaluation of the CHMI has been funded through 2010 to compare outcomes in the CHMI communities with outcomes in comparison communities that are well matched to the project sites. The study focuses on evaluation of community-level approaches to encourage changes in norms that increase support for healthy marriages.

In 2006, with funds provided under the Deficit Reduction Act of 2005, an estimated $4 million, was made available for responsible fatherhood, marriage, and family strengthening grants for incarcerated fathers and their partners. The program supports services to promote or sustain healthy marriage primarily to unmarried couples or married couples where one parent is incarcerated or has been recently released from prison or jail or is on probation or parole. The Office of the Assistant Secretary for Planning and Evaluation (ASPE) in DHSS will support an evaluation of the performance of these grants. Technical assistance will be provided to grantees that need help in complying with evaluation requirements.

Work

Like marriage, strong ties to work can lead to desistance from crime. One study using longitudinal data found that job stability was strongly related to desistance from crime (Sampson and Laub, 1993). In a similar vein, a study using qualitative data showed that acquiring a satisfying job was an important contingency in the lives of men who desisted from crime (Shover, 1996). However, as in the case of marriage, the nature of the relationship between work and desistance is not known: it is possible that "selection effects" are affecting that link: some factor or factors that predispose persons to find and remain in stable employment may also predispose them to desist from crime.

One of the most convincing attempts to counteract selection bias comes from an analysis of data from a national work experiment that drew participants from poor urban neighborhoods in nine U.S. cities. Overall, the people who were given jobs through the experiment showed no reduction in crime relative to those in a control group (Uggen, 2000). However, age significantly interacted with employment to affect the timing of illegal earnings and arrest. Participants aged 27 or older were more likely to desist when provided with even marginal employment. For younger participants, the experimental job treatment had no effect on desistance. The findings from Uggen (2000) are important because the experimental nature of the data addresses the selectivity issue that has plagued much of the research on desistance. By specifying event history models accounting for assignment to, eligibility for, and participation in the National Supported Work Demonstration Project, this study provides more refined estimates of the effects of work as a turning point in the lives of offenders. Unfortunately, data for this study were collected from 1975-1979. Given changes in labor markets since the 1970s and current employment prospects for uneducated whites and minorities, the finding that work is a turning point may also be outdated.

More recently, Rossman and Roman (2003), in their evaluation of the Opportunities to Succeed (OPTS) Program, found that full-time employment among releasees increased with greater interaction with case managers and with higher levels of participation in drug treatment programs and that an increase in levels of employment was a predictor of reductions in drug dealing, violent crime, and property crime.

Bloom (2006) notes that there have been few rigorous studies of recent, employee-focused reentry models. A similar conclusion is reached by Visher, Winterfield, and Coggeshall (2005). New models of work programs for releasees, such as the Safer Foundation's Ready4Work model that is also being tested by the U.S. Department of Labor, focus on providing coordinated services both before and after an inmate is released. Evaluations of such models show results that are only somewhat positive.

DESISTANCE AND PAROLE

For individual offenders, the major functions of imprisonment are retribution, removing dangerous people from the community, rehabilitation, and specific deterrence of future offending after release. The goals of parole supervision are similar and can be broadly conceived as "service" and "surveillance": the rehabilitation of releasees and facilitation of their reentry in a community and the deterrence of crime and crime-related behaviors. In this framework, parole then serves as a sorting function by identifying releasees who fail quickly and returning them to prison in order to protect communities and by making services available to those who might most benefit from them. Successful reintegration of offenders protects the communities in which they reside. Thus, the purposes of parole supervision are more utilitarian, integrative, and rehabilitative than the purposes of incarceration; retribution recedes into the background.

Understanding the possible links between desistance from crime and community reintegration has important implications for designing correctional policies, especially parole. One strategy is the greater use of community-based corrections in order to assist offenders in their reintegration in a community. According to a life-course theory of age-graded informal social control (Sampson and Laub, 1993), effective sanctions should include methods of building social bonds to family, employment, and the community when offenders are released from prison. That is, they would combine treatment and services that promote connections with the community with appropriate emphasis on surveillance.

Emphasizing the importance of treatment and services for the reduction of criminal behavior does not mean that community safety need be compromised. Community corrections strategies can provide effective surveillance and control of offenders to maintain the safety of a community while avoiding the placement of offenders in the potentially criminogenic environment of prison, an example of which is found in a recent study by Bhati (2007). For a sample of prisoners released from state prisons in 1994, Bhati used preincarceration arrest patterns to construct anticipated postrelease offending trajectories. A comparison of these counterfactuals with the actual postrelease offending patterns suggests that about 4 percent more returned to offending than was projected (i.e., they had a criminogenic experience in prison). Overall, 40 percent were deterred from future offending (i.e., were not rearrested after release), while the majority (56%), were merely incapacitated, that is, neither deterred nor rehabilitated by incarceration since they were found to revert back to anticipated offending patterns. Program components aimed at improving informal social controls and providing social support may reduce such criminal behavior, thus reducing the need for future incarceration or surveillance of releasees (see Laub and Allen, 1999). Moreover, community sanctions can promote offender accountability to their victims and to the community at large. In a paper presented at the workshop, Taxman (2006) notes that recent literature in the field has highlighted the way that natural support systems and informal social controls can augment and enhance the formal social controls imposed by correctional agencies. Informal social controls may encourage people to commit to a prosocial life-style and to develop new networks that include law-abiding citizens, not only through employment and families, but also through other types of community engagement, such as participating in the work of neighborhood associations or volunteer work (see also Uggen and Manza, 2004).

In the long run, if involvement in serious crime and delinquency automatically curtails future opportunities, releasees will have fewer incentives and options to desist and lead conventional lives. Many new laws in effect have permanently disenfranchised ex-offenders from employment opportunities, housing assistance, welfare benefits, and political rights (see Petersilia, 2003; Travis, 2005; Manza and Uggen, 2006). Such policies serve as barriers for ex-offenders to reconnect to the institutions that have been demonstrated as important in the desistance process, especially work and family. Thus, current policies regarding ex-offenders may produce unintended criminogenic effects by further damaging offenders' already weak social bonds and cutting them off from promising avenues for desistance and reintegration into communities.

WHO OFFENDS? WHO DESISTS?

There are multiple pathways and factors involved in desistance from crime, including marriage and work, as noted above. Transformation of personal identify—that is, cognitive change as a precursor to behavioral change—has also been documented (Maruna, 2001; Giordano et al., 2002). Reduced exposure to delinquent peers fosters desistance from crime for youthful offenders (Warr, 1998). Perhaps the most obvious and simplest pathway to desistance from crime is aging: offending declines with age for all offenses (Glueck and Glueck, 1974; Gottfredson and Hirschi, 1990; Laub and Sampson, 2003). However, in spite of the evidence to date, interventions designed to help men and women desist from criminal behavior have been slow to target these factors, with the exception of those related to employment—job readiness, training, and placement programs. Such programs are easier to implement than programs concerned with marriage and family and peer associations.

One factor that appears to increase desistance from crime is reduced consumption of illegal drugs. The Federal Bureau of Prisons Office of Research and Evaluation (2000) evaluated its residential drug treatment program, which includes a transitional component that keeps former prisoners engaged in treatment as they return to their home communities. A rigorous research design included three methodologies to account for selection bias. More than 2,000 individuals were included in the research. After 3 years, treatment subjects were significantly less likely to be rearrested or have their parole revoked, than the control subjects (52% and 44%) and less likely to use drugs (58% and 50%). These results mean reduction in recidivism of about 16 percent. Arrests for all offenders also showed differences. Employment rates showed no differences. Moreover, in a 12-year follow-up of a sample of cocaine-dependent releasees, Hser and colleagues (2006) found that men who were continually abstinent for at least 5 years reported less past year involvement in crime, unemployment, and abuse of other substances than those who continued to use cocaine.

Other factors have also been proposed as important in the desistance process. With regard to education, Locher and Moretti (2004) found that education decreases arrest and incarceration, based on prisoner, arrest, and self-report data. Other factors for which there is little or mixed evidence include residential change, religion, criminal justice sanctions, criminal justice supervision (probation and parole), and a wide range of correctional and community interventions.

THE PROCESS OF INDIVIDUAL CHANGE

There is remarkable heterogeneity in criminal offending. Some offenders have short careers in one or a variety of crimes; other offenders have very long careers. A few specialize in one type of criminal activity, while most appear to commit a variety of crimes. From a theoretical perspective, rather than thinking in the simplistic 0-1 categories of offenders and nonoffenders, it is useful to view criminality as following a path consisting of one or more crime and noncrime cycles (Glaser, 1969). Research on ex-offenders has shown that men typically do not commit crimes continually for long periods of time: instead, they "follow a zig-zag path . . . going from non crime to crime and to non crime again. Sometimes this sequence is repeated many times, but sometimes they clearly go to crime only once; sometimes these shifts are for long duration or even permanent, and sometimes they are short lived" (Glaser, 1969, p. 58; see also Piquero, 2004).

Processes of desistance have emerged that are common across a variety of problem behavior areas, including crime (Fagan, 1989). First, the decision to stop appears to be preceded by a variety of negative consequences, both formal and informal, such as a prison sentence or the loss of a job. Second, multiple processes appear to be involved in sustaining and reinforcing the decision to change. Research on alcoholism, smoking, and obesity show commonalities in a process of three basic stages of behavior change:

motivation and commitment, initial behavior change, and maintenance of change (Brownell et al., 1986). Given this pattern, a realistic goal for ex-offenders, especially for high-rate offenders released from prison, is not zero offending, but reduced offending (reduced in terms of frequency and seriousness) and increased lengths of nonoffending periods. Empirical research on desistance has consistently demonstrated that this goal can be achieved.[2]

There appears to be an important distinction between lapses (slips) and relapse, and much could be learned about the processes of change if more were known about which slips lead to relapses and which do not (Brownell et al., 1986). There is some evidence to suggest that the determinants of lapses are different from the determinants of relapses. For instance, lapses are more commonly associated with situational factors, and relapses are related to individual factors such as negative emotional states or stress events (Brownell et al., 1986). It would also be valuable to know more about the timing of lapses in the change process, how this process applies to desistance from crime, and how it operates in a context of severe official sanctions, such as reincarceration, which typically are not part of the dynamics of behavioral change for addictive disorders.

What is most important from this perspective is that the goal of desistance programs is not necessarily zero offending, but less offending and less serious offending. Less crime does not mean no crime: it is important for policy makers and program administrators to have realistic goals and to have forms of punishments and rewards available that will support those realistic goals.

DESISTANCE PROGRAMS

Kinds of Analysis

Programs to encourage desistance from crime have both advantages and disadvantages, including budgetary costs. A cost-benefit analysis is one standard way to assess programs. In doing so, however, one must keep in mind that the benefits of a desistance program are often not confined to reductions in criminality. Similarly, post-incarceration programs and policies not specifically aimed at reducing recidivism—such as those for drug treatment, mental health care, adult education, job training, and measures to increase the effective market wages for low-skilled labor—may result in desistance as a benefit. For example, with regard to substance abuse, re-

---

[2]For an extensive review, see Laub and Sampson (2001) and citations therein. In addition, see Laub and Sampson (2003), Sampson and Laub (2003), Sampson, Laub, and Wimer (2006), and Ezell and Cohen (2005).

search has found that nonusers are less likely to return to prison (Wexler et al., 1999). However a program is labeled and by whatever agency it is run, good policy analysis considers all of its benefits (advantages) and compares them with all of its costs (disadvantages).

Economists' standard measure for assessing the nonfinancial benefits and costs of a program is "willingness to pay": how much the beneficiaries of a program would be willing to pay from their own resources for the advantage it generates for them, and how much the people disadvantaged by that program would have to be paid to compensate them for the disadvantages (see Cook and Ludwig, 2000 and the references cited therein; Cohen et al., 2004; Nagin et al., 2006). For example, the merely financial losses to crime victims (e.g., the value of stolen property, medical expenses, lost wages) do not exhaust the social costs of crime and thus the benefits of crime control. Victims also experience pain and suffering, and even persons not yet victimized incur costs to avoid crime (e.g., by staying indoors or by moving) and suffer anxiety about the risk of crime. Moreover, the costs of crime-avoidance behaviors are not restricted to those who engage in them: when a drugstore restricts its hours or moves out of a neighborhood because of the owner's fear of crime, residents of that neighborhood lose both their convenience as shoppers and economic opportunity as potential employees. The relevant question, from a policymaker's perspective, is what a reduction in the risk of victimization is worth to those who enjoy it: for example, how much more rent would a person be prepared to pay to live in a lower crime neighborhood, all else being equal?

Different programs compete for scarce resources: dollars, staff, managerial and political attention, and even office space. In allocating funds to increase desistance (or for any other purpose), one can also ask which of the two or more programs makes the greatest contribution to the specific goal for each dollar or other resource unit. This analytic approach is known as cost effectiveness.

These two styles of analysis—cost benefit and cost effectiveness—do not exhaust the full range of considerations that might go into the choice of public programs. For example, they exclude any consideration of justice or fairness. Nonetheless, they both provide useful guidance when the appropriate data are available and can serve as conceptual frameworks for thinking about programs, even when, as is often the case, those data are not available.

For example, current correctional budgets are highly skewed toward institutional corrections (prisons and jails) in comparison with community corrections (probation and parole). A cost-effectiveness analysis would ask how many crimes (weighted for severity) could be prevented by adding $1 million to an institutional corrections budget (enough to keep approximately 40 prisoners for an additional year) in comparison with adding that same $1 million for more intensive community supervision (enough to monitor 125 high-risk parolees in the community).

To consider the example, suppose that the average prisoner would have, if released, five times the criminal activity rate (lambda) of the average high-risk probationer and that doubling probation supervision would cut crime among high-risk probationers by 10 percent. If the lambda of the high-risk probationer is x, incarceration would prevent 40 ($5x$) crimes per year, or $200x$ crimes, while intensive probation supervision would prevent 0.1 ($1,000x$) crimes per year, or $100x$ crimes. Thus, with the stated assumptions, prison is more cost-effective as crime control than probation. But, if intensifying probation would cut crime among high-risk probationers by 30 percent, intensive probation would be a more cost-effective use of that $1 million. It should be noted that this analysis can be done without monetizing the costs of crime (the benefits of crime control).[3]

In contrast, if the decision facing a lawmaker is whether to add $1 million to the corrections budget, there is a different set of questions than those above. One would need to know how much crime that sum would prevent, the value of that reduction to potential victims, and the nonbudget costs and non-crime-reduction benefits associated with that expenditure.

Assessing Programs

In thinking about how to assess desistance programs, it is critically important to keep in mind the heterogeneity of the population of released offenders: from those who have committed one nonviolent offense to those who may have served more than one sentence in prison for multiple violent offenses. Programs that may work for one kind of parolee may not work or even be appropriate to try for other groups. As but one example, Piquero and Pogarsky (2002) has argued that the threat of sanctions would be most ineffective on the two extremes of the offending spectrum, that is, those who either have extremely high self-control and those with very low self-control. Moreover, even for appropriate programs, poor program implementation is often a barrier to both program effectiveness and to program evaluation.

It is useful to think of the two obstacles (heterogeneity and implementation) in terms of the "demand" and "supply" for rehabilitation. Limited demand, that is resistance to change among parolees, limits what even the

---

[3]By contrast with cost-benefit analysis, cost-effectiveness analysis necessarily ignores important ancillary questions, such as the value to victims of having the perpetrators punished with incarceration rather than probation or the damage to prisoners and their families from incarceration.

most carefully implemented program can achieve, while limits on supply—the state-of-the-art in providing rehabilitative services—puts a cap on what can be achieved even by programs aimed at parolees amenable to change.

On the demand side, an important and often ignored dimension of heterogeneity among released prisoners is first release. As noted in Chapter 1, inmates released from their first prison sentence have lower recidivism rates than those released from prison for the second, third, or fourth time. A recent study found that prisoners released for the first time accumulated 18-25 percent fewer arrests during the first 3 years out of prison than those who had been to prison and released at least once before—controlling for sex, age, race, imprisonment offense, prior arrests, and time served (Rosenfeld et al., 2005). Over time, the fraction of released prisoners who are first-timers has declined, while the fraction who have are being released from their second or other incarceration has increased. This distinction is important (Tonry, 2004, p. 189):

> . . . most people sent to prison, and hence released, will be persistent offenders, and accordingly . . . on average people released from prison will present relatively high risks for recidivism. . . . Is it not odd . . . that in our time, we have forgotten the lower risk first-timers, and *do not even think in our research to ask separately about them* [emphasis added]

By not distinguishing first-timers from the repeat offenders —who have shown that they are more difficult candidates for reentry—supervision and reentry programs may be doomed from the start. Approaches that work with the first-timers may not work with the repeaters and so may seriously affect assessment outcomes of desistance programs.

3

Parole: Current Practices

Since the 1970s, the focus of parole supervision has shifted from the dual purposes of making sure that parolees complied with their conditions of parole and aiding their social reintegration by providing community resources (e.g., job training, drug counseling) to a more direct emphasis on crime control. Parole agents increasingly emphasize their police function and deemphasize the casework portion of their role (Petersilia, 2003; Solomon, Kachnowski, and Bhati, 2005); yet there is wide variation across agencies. This chapter discusses the most recent evidence on the nature, costs, and effectiveness of parole supervision and services for releasees in the community.

SUPERVISORY AGENCIES AND PERSONNEL

Supervision

Parole "supervision" is an unfortunate term because it means different things in different parole settings. Although parolees' behavior is sometimes closely monitored, frequently it is not. An expansion of "intensive supervision parole" and the use of new technologies, such as electronic monitoring and a global positioning system (GPS), have occurred during the past 20 years as part of a broader movement to focus supervision and treatment resources on those either the most likely to benefit or those in greatest danger of recidivism (Petersilia, 2003). These approaches do enhance the capacity of officials to monitor parolees; however, they are not used, and likely cannot be used, for most parolees.

Supervision for many parolees consists of simply checking in with the parole agency. Such checking in varies from mailing in a form to a parole officer, to a periodic phone call to a clerical staff person, to a face-to-face visit with a parole agent. In a keynote address before the Corrections Technology Association, the director of the New York City Probation Services described that agency's automated check-in procedure with regard to probationers, most of whom never have been to prison (Horn, 2002, p. 3).

> Several years ago, New York Probation pioneered the use of "reporting kiosks," which were touted in TECHBEAT as one of the most innovative uses of technology in community corrections. In fact, today, 15,000 probationers, over 1/3 of my active caseload, "report" to a kiosk. What does this mean? Probationers come to our downtown "fortress probation" offices where they wait on long lines in overheated offices to stand in front of an ATM-like device, really no more than a PC in a hardened case. Then, using a biometric hand scanner and PIN their identity is verified and they respond on a touch screen to a series of questions similar to those most often asked by probation officers. If all is in order they are provided a receipt and a new date to come in.

For most parolees, on the other hand, supervision means check-ins, combined with periodic field contacts by a parole agent with the parolee and his associates (called collateral contacts). Field contacts range between once a week to once every few months. Petersilia (2006) reported that nearly one in four California parolees is assigned to minimum supervision, meaning that they see a parole officer only twice a year. Another 43 percent of parolees fall within the control services classification, meaning that they will see a parole officer once every 6 weeks (Petersilia, 2001). For other parolees, more frequent contact is most likely immediately after release or when there are problems; less frequent contact is more likely with parolees who have long periods left on a parole sentence and good, stable behavior. Field contacts take place at the residence of parolees, their workplaces, or elsewhere. Ideally, these are surprise visits, but this is not always possible.

The purpose of the contacts is to make sure that parolees are complying with their conditions of parole. As noted above, parolees are expected to comply with a standard set of conditions—do not violate any law, do not possess a firearm or illegal drugs, do not associate with persons with criminal records, do not leave the jurisdiction, etc.—and some parolees have additional conditions, such as required drug treatment, required participation in other programs such as job training and drug testing. Although some contacts may essentially be counseling sessions, others may be conducted solely to ensure that the parolee is working regularly or to collect a urine sample for drug testing. Collateral contacts may also be made with the police, family members, employers, social service providers, school officials, or even neighbors. With check-in systems, parole officers rely on collateral contacts to verify that parolees are complying with conditions of release. The average parole caseload in the United States is 70 parolees to one parole officer.

Officers with caseloads under "intensive supervision" are responsible for fewer parolees (about 30), allowing more frequent contacts on the assumption that closer supervision will act as a greater deterrent because of the high likelihood of detecting more violations. In addition to more frequent contacts, individuals subject to intensive supervision parole frequently have special parole conditions (e.g., frequent drug testing, therapeutic drug treatment, electronic monitoring). Some parolees are placed on intensive supervision parole on the basis of a number of available classification schemes. One is a Salient Factor Score, which is determined by an offender's criminal history and prison adjustment; another is the Client Management Classification System (for reviews, see Harris et al., 2004; Lattimore, 2006). Other parolees may be assigned to intensive supervision because of the severity of their most recent offense conviction or for particular types of offenses.

The main objective of intensive supervision parole is a reduction in recidivism for new crimes, but the available evidence suggests that this objective has not yet been achieved. A rigorous study by Petersilia and Turner (1993) of intensive supervision parole and probation programs in nine states, found that offenders in intensive supervision programs had relatively the same number of subsequent arrests, but more technical violations and returns to incarceration, than their nonintensive supervision program counterparts. However, if those programs combined drug treatment, community service, and employment programs with surveillance, recidivism rates were 10 to 20 percent lower than for those who did not participate in such activities. A meta-analysis of intensive supervision probation and parole programs also found that combining surveillance with treatment resulted in reduced recidivism (Gendreau and Little, 1993).

Electronic monitoring is used in some jurisdictions to complement or in lieu of traditional parole supervision. If a parolee leaves the area to which he or she is restricted, a signal is sent to a monitoring office or computer system. Again, in contrast to expectations and general belief, research shows that individuals on probation with electronic monitoring are no more or less likely to experience new arrests than those under standard supervision (Finn and Muirhead-Steves, 2002). Whether this would be the case with parolees is an empirical question.

Intensive supervision parole, with or without electronic monitoring, is more expensive than traditional parole supervision: about $8,000 and

$5,000, respectively, per year (Petersilia, 2003), compared to about $2,000 for traditional supervision. Yet the annual cost of intensive supervision and electronic monitoring are less than the cost of prison, which averages $23,397 per year per prisoner in the United States (Petersilia, 2006). Conceptually, electronic monitoring could be expected to enhance enforcement of stay away orders, curfews and participation in social services and could enable the monitoring of many other conditions for release to the community.

Caseloads

A belief that smaller caseloads would lead to less offending dates back at least to 1973, when the President's Commission on Law Enforcement and the Administration of Justice recommended that parole and probation caseloads not exceed 35 individuals. During the early 1970s, the U.S. Department of Health, Education, and Welfare (now the Department of Health and Human Services) provided support to reduce some specialized caseloads (welfare recipients and parolees with alcohol and drug dependencies) to 25. Today, the increased size of the prison population, with consequent increases in the number of releasees returning to communities, and unchanged levels of funding for parole services, have led to caseloads that are often at 70 or higher (Petersilia, 2001).[1]

Although caseload size has not been shown to affect recidivism among parolees, one can assume that caseload sizes are not limitless: neither effective supervision nor treatment is as likely when the number of persons being supervised overwhelms the capacity of parole officers and agents. Although the argument for focusing resources simply on caseload size has not been supported, it is possible that very large caseloads diminish the effectiveness of other strategies. Moreover, it has been shown that caseload size is a significant factor in determining how parole officers deliver services and how they experience their jobs (Quinn and Gould, 2003). It is likely that the quality of assessment and classification and the effectiveness of social services and treatments provided are more important than the size of caseloads. With this in mind, the American Probation and Parole Association has recommended a workload model in determining the size of caseloads (see caseload standards at http://www.appa-net.org/ccheadlines/docs/caseloads_standards_pp_0906.p [accessed July 2007]).

---

[1]For comparison, probation caseloads are frequently much higher, exceeding 200 or even 300 in some jurisdictions. Although on average probationers have committed less serious offences than parolees, this is not always true: probationers may include people convicted of such serious offenses as robbery, assault, domestic violence, and drug-related crimes. Many are in need of significant treatment or intensive supervision.

Parole Agencies' Missions

Community protection is a common goal of parole agents, but the route to this objective varies. At one extreme are agencies that define the primary goal of parole supervision as surveillance and the control and regulation of their clients' behavior. At the other extreme are agencies that attempt to protect the public by providing the treatment and reintegration services that are believed to promote desistance. Obviously, most parole agencies lie on a continuum between these extremes; specific offices and individual parole agents define their responsibilities at various places along this continuum. Agents are influenced by the culture of their offices, which can change over time. The culture of parole agencies is an important factor in how parole supervision is carried out (McCleary, 1992)

The overall shift towards a crime control model of parole in recent decades and variations across agencies in how they define their mission create a challenge for some reforms when they do not align with an agency, an office, or agents' cultures. For example, if a new treatment regime is tried in an agency that is primarily focused on surveillance, parole agents may be less likely to implement the treatment as the treatment designers and even their supervisors intend.

Parole Agents: Conflicting Missions

Variations in agency mission and culture—as well as in the fundamental role of parole itself—point to the conflict for parole agents: they don't know whether they are expected to be law enforcement agents or social caseworkers. They have responsibility for enforcing the law and the conditions of parole, as well as assisting in released offenders' reintegration in society. In part, the resolution of this conflict in favor of enforcement has been driven by heinous events—such as sexual assault, as in the Willie Horton case, or the rape and murder of a child, as in the Polly Klass and Megan Kanka cases. Media coverage of these kinds of crimes, the crime victims' movement which took off in the early 1980s, and the war on drugs have all fueled a trend toward punitiveness. The cost of strict enforcement, whether warranted or not, is borne only by the parolee. The cost of failing to clamp down on a dangerous parolee is borne by an entire agency or, as in the Willie Horton case, a governor. Consequently, agencies have been hard pressed to emphasize rehabilitation or take the process of relapse into account.

The agents who emphasize the supervision role typically think of themselves as, and act like, corrections officers whose job is to maintain control of their charges. Theirs is a workday of surveillance, investigation, and enforcement. The agents who emphasize the casework side of the role tend to define the parolees on their caseloads as clients in need of problem diagnostics and appropriate services. The conflict is that nearly all parole officers are called on by their employers to do both. They sometimes find themselves derided as "detective lite" by law enforcement colleagues and chided for being a "social worker with a gun" by social workers and other treatment professionals.

In some jurisdictions these conflicts have been minimized by changing the institutional positioning of the parole functions. Some jurisdictions have turned to or partnered with law enforcement to buttress the supervision of parolees. The Washington State Department of Corrections, in its neighborhood corrections initiative, has assigned corrections officers to ride with police in what is known on the streets of Seattle as the "jump out van."[2] The teams proactively patrol the streets, working exclusively in transient, urban, and homeless areas to provide an unparalleled level of supervision of releasees and a bridge to services ranging from drug treatment and housing to socks, food, water, and shelter (Northwest Law Enforcement and Public Safety Training, 2006).

While parole (and probation) officers formerly were drawn heavily from the ranks of retired police officers, they are now usually college graduates who define themselves as professional parole (or probation) officers. Starting salaries are similar to those for public school teachers and, as in teaching, their supervisors worry about burnout. Working conditions for parole agents can be difficult: large caseloads, less than agreeable clients, a lot of time in the least desirable parts of communities, and plenty of blame when a parolee commits a new crime.

Police and Parole Supervision

Parole officers and local police agencies have long had close informal working relationships. In some jurisdictions the police are routinely notified when a person is released on parole in their area. Many parole officers regularly scan the arrest logs of police departments to see if parolees on their caseloads were picked up. Historically, this task was simply defined as doing the job.

More recently, more formalized partnerships between parole and probation agencies and police departments have sometimes been set up. As a retired chief probation officer noted (Burrell, 2005, p. 596):

> Ironically, line officers have been collaborating for years—with police officers, drug counselors, teachers, psychologists, employment specialists and others—who were also involved with their clients. The critical differ-

---

[2]Washington has abolished traditional parole although there is intensive supervision for some released offenders.

ence today is that these partnerships are forged at a higher level and are more formal.

The Urban Institute recently published an excellent report summarizing several ongoing law enforcement programs designed to positively affect prisoner reentry (La Vigne et al., 2006).

While parole officers in some agencies may arrest individuals, particularly for noncriminal violations of specific parole conditions, other officers may elect to have sworn police officers make such arrests, and some agencies require it. Federal probation and parole officers are, by policy, directed not to execute warrants.

RULES FOR RELEASEES

The goal of parole supervision (or other forms of supervised release) is to enable and require prison releasees to live law-abiding lives in the community. As just discussed, both services and supervision are part of parole. Supervision includes rules, and rules necessarily have sanctions for violations. A key question in enforcing rules in any situation is the role of incentives and disincentives: What is the proper balance between incentives to reward good behavior and sanctions to punish bad behavior? Since the ultimate goal of parole supervision is to prevent releasees from committing new offenses, the rules of parole should be demonstrably linked to reducing the risk of new offenses. Unfortunately, we know little from research about whether rules of parole are linked to less offending (Solomon et al., 2005).

A major issue in parole involves violations of the specific conditions of parole (the parole contract) that do not involve criminal offenses. Such violations include meeting with known felons, missing a check-in or meeting with a parole agent, being out after a curfew time, and missing a scheduled drug test. One view is that such violations should not have major consequences, such as return to prison. In this view, unless there is a pattern of violations or absconding from supervision that signals a releasee's refusal to take the supervision relationship seriously, parole sanctions need not, and in general, should not involve revocation of parole and return to prison. (This approach does not involve conduct that would be prosecuted if committed by an ordinary citizen, though presumably that would be a new offense.) The underlying assumption of this approach is that less drastic sanctions, if delivered quickly and predictably, can control a parolee's behavior and enhance the prospects for long-term success.

The contrary view is that some violations, even of a procedural nature, are significant signs that a parolee is not respecting the terms of the parole contract—is not attempting to live as a law-abiding citizen—and so should suffer major consequences. This can be characterized as analogous to the "broken windows" approach to law enforcement, because it rests on the assumption that minor violations, if left unattended, can lead to more serious ones (Wilson and Kelling, 1982; Cartier, Farabee, and Pendergast, 2006).

Tracking violations can be complex because of large caseloads. Many parolees meet with their parole officer on an infrequent basis, so detection of violations may seem almost random. But officers have broad discretion in most cases in the way they supervise their caseloads. They can give specific parolees that worry them more attention. Research indicates that parolees who are more closely supervised have higher violation rates.

Many behaviors that involve compliance with the rules of parole can be the subject of the supervision process. Abstinence from illicit drug use can be monitored by chemical testing. For releasees with established drug problems, testing can be frequent enough (i.e., twice a week) to leave little or no window for undetected drug use. At that frequency, tests can be scheduled in advance, making them less disruptive to parolees' lives. Parolees without known drug problems and those who have proven their ability to refrain from drug use by a long series of negative tests can be monitored by random testing. These approaches are in contrast to the practice of infrequent testing on announced dates, which can be virtually an open invitation to use drugs other than in the few days before the scheduled test. For those parolees subject to frequent testing, the efficacy of the threat of sanctions in reducing drug use is greatly enhanced by the use of testing methods that provide on-the-spot results. Other parole rules—such as curfews, stay-away orders, and requirements to appear at work or for treatment—can be verified by electronic monitoring.

The level of contentiousness that sometimes characterizes this debate over violating specified conditions of parole may be lessened by combining realistic and enforceable release conditions with graduated incentives and consequences (i.e., graduated responses). For example, Andrews and Bonta (1998) and Taxman (2006) specifically discuss the importance of using rewards in the process as a means of encouraging compliance with program requirements.

Positive incentives for compliance are important complements to sanctions for violations. Less intrusive supervision and the remission of previously collected fines are both likely to be valued by releasees, but a wide variety of rewards, such as tickets to sporting events, may also have a role. The benefits of even small reductions in recidivism can easily cover the costs of such rewards; the greater challenge may be in devising the rewards and justifying them to policy makers and the public.

4

Services and Programs for Releasees

Recent research on desistance from crime has generated a body of knowledge that examines the underlying conditions that lead to less frequent or a declining rate toward zero offending; yet programs and services for parolees are, in general, not based on these findings, but are instead rooted in the research on individual behavioral change. Farrall and Maruna (2004) have noted that only recently have there been attempts to link findings from desistance studies with evaluations of offender management programs and policies. Part of the problem is that both theory development and research on the mechanisms underlying desistance are limited. We do not know, for example, how individual change and social circumstances such as marriage or work interact to produce desistance.

Because the committee believes these unexplored issues are important, we try to provide something of a baseline of information about these linkages by organizing parts of this chapter on programs and services for releases in a desistance framework. For example, in a longitudinal study on probation and desistance (Farrall, 2002), the researchers found employment and family relationship experiences were more critical to successful desistance than differences in probation practice. The desistance literature on parolees has found similar results, though the reasons for them are poorly understood. Using a desistance framework makes it possible to focus on the purpose of the intervention rather than on offending and allows consideration of the broader context required to support behavioral change (Farrall and Maruna, 2004). Although the disconnect between these literatures may make this framework seem forced at times, we believe it fosters the development of a more coherent structure for future research and policy development.

There is an overlap between conditions that promote desistance and the individual effects of change but it is not clear where that intersection lies. Does individual change provide a basis for employment and a stable marriage, or do a stable marriage and a job provide the context for individual change? Intervention research has shown that the most successful programs fostering individual change and leading to desistance are those that start in prison and then continue in the community setting once an individual is released.

The chapter begins with a review of research findings on interventions that are offered either before or after release from prison, organized in a desistance framework that includes education and employment, marriage, drug treatment, and individual change. This is followed by a section on current innovations in reentry programming, including prerelease planning and the consequences of early failure. The third section considers available services and their effects, including physical and mental health services, mentoring programs, and best practices.

RESEARCH ON PROGRAMS

Education and Employment

In the United States, adult corrections facilities have a long history of providing education and vocational training as part of the rehabilitation process (Piehl, 1998; Gaes et al., 1999), based on the belief that improving education and job skills will promote desistance. However, participation in these programs has been declining since the early 1990s: among soon-to-be-released prisoners in 1991, 42 percent reported participating in education programs and 31 percent in vocational programs; in 1997 the figures were 35 percent and 27 percent, respectively (Lynch and Sabol, 2001). The reasons for these declines include the rapid growth in the prison population, decreased state and federal funding for in-prison programs, the frequent transfers of prisoners from one facility to another, and greater interest in short-term programs, such as substance abuse and cognitive-behavioral programs (Lawrence et al., 2002).

Some studies show that recidivism rates are significantly lower for releasees with more education (MacKenzie, 2006; Adams et al., 1994; Boudin, 1993; Harer, 1995; Stillman, 1999, Fabelo, 2000). Moreover, comprehensive reviews of dozens of individual program evaluations generally conclude that adult academic and vocational programs lead to reduced recidivism (MacKenzie, 2006) and increased employment of 5-10 percent (Gerber and Fritsch, 1994; Gaes et al., 1999; Cullen and Gendreau, 2000;

Wilson et al., 2000; Aos et al., 2006). However, the majority of the evaluations are of poor quality, and a close examination of their methodological problems reduces confidence in their results (MacKenzie, 2006; Wilson et al., 2000)

For correctional education programming to be successful, it must be part of a systematic approach that includes programs for employability, social skills training, and other specialized programming (Taxman, 1998). Best-practice correctional education programs are both carefully tailored to individual prisoners and related to vocational and job skills training. Education and job training for prisoners who were low earners are most successful when they provide workers with credentials that meet private-sector demands. Programs that provide training, a range of services and supports, incentives, and access to better employers work well, especially when there are strong incentives for releasees to get jobs (Holzer and Martinson, 2005; Visher and Courtney, 2006).

To be most effective, inmate screening, needs assessment, and the provision of services need to be integrated, but this approach may run counter to other institutional priorities. In many systems, security classification takes precedence over other activities, which may affect the organization of and availability of services. Many prisoners would like to enroll in education and training programs but slots are not available or they are not eligible because of their security status or short sentence length. If the highest need prisoners are also the highest risk offenders, it might make sense to shift some programming resources to higher security institutions where such prisoners are concentrated (Logan, 1993).

As noted above, work is a primary feature of successful reintegration and desistance (Sampson and Laub, 1990, 1993; Nagin and Waldfogel, 1998). The time spent and connections made at work probably serve as informal social controls that prevent criminal behavior. Having a job, especially a good job, reduces the economic incentive for criminal behavior. For example, using data from the 1980 National Longitudinal Survey of Youth, economist Jeffrey Grogger (1998) has estimated that the elasticity of crime participation with respect to wages is −1.0, two and a half times higher than the elasticity provided by incarceration.[1] Specifically he found that a 10 percent increase in wages would reduce crime participation by 6–9 percent. His estimates suggest that young men's behavior is very responsive to price incentives and that falling real wages for youth may have been partially responsible for the rise in youth crime during the 1980s and early 1990s.

Finding employment is one of the most pressing problems that releasees

---

[1]Elasticity is the ratio of the proportional change in one variable with respect to proportional change in another variable.

face. Although two-thirds of former prisoners were working prior to their imprisonment (Maguire, 1994), their educational level, work experience, and skills are well below national averages for the general population (Andrews and Bonta, 1994; Petersilia, 2005). Moreover, the stigma and legal restrictions associated with incarceration often make it difficult for ex-prisoners to secure employment (Holzer et al., 2002; Bushway and Reuter, 2002). When releasees do find jobs, they tend to earn less than employees with similar background characteristics who have not been in prison (Bushway and Reuter, 2002). Thus, research supports a strong programmatic emphasis on increasing prisoners' and releasees' employability, through skills training, job readiness, and, possibly, work-release programs during incarceration and after release.

The U.S. Department of Labor (DOL) has a long history of evaluating community-based work programs for former prisoners and people with criminal records, beginning with several large evaluations of job training and financial support for former prisoners in the 1970s. The LIFE and TARP studies conducted in the 1970s are well known (see Rossi, Berk, and Lenihan, 1980). These programs offered ex-offenders varying levels of unemployment compensation and job placement assistance. Random assignment studies in Texas, Georgia, and Baltimore found that income supports reduced property crimes although they also created a disincentive for ex-offenders to find employment (Berk et al., 1980).

Other DOL-funded job training initiatives that included ex-offenders were the National Supported Work Demonstration, Job Corps, JobStart, and the Job Training Partnership Act. More recently, DOL has funded faith- or other community-based organizations in 30 sites under the Prisoner Reentry Initiative for employment services and job placements, specifically for clients with nonviolent histories (with varying definitions by site) who are under the supervision of the criminal justice system.

The most recent random assignment study, initiated in 1994, evaluated the Opportunity to Succeed Program, which delivered employment services within a set of comprehensive services for drug-using former prisoners. The study found that participants were more likely to be employed full time in the year after release, and they reported less drug use; however, self-reports of arrests and official record measures of recidivism showed no differences between participants and controls (Rossman and Roman, 2003).

A meta-analysis that examined the effects of employment training and job assistance in the community for ex-offenders concluded that such programs are responsible for a modest, but significant, 5 percent reduction in recidivism (Aos et al., 2006). However, another meta-analysis, using a very similar, but not identical set of studies and methods, concluded that community-based employment programs do not significantly reduce recidivism for ex-offenders (Visher, Winterfield, and Coggeshall, 2005).[2] Thus, although work programs can have a significant effect on the employment and recidivism rates of male releasees (Bushway and Reuter, 2002), the effect sizes may be small.

Current job assistance and training programs for former prisoners—such as the Center for Employment Opportunities (New York), Safer Foundation (Chicago), and Project Rio (Texas)—are more comprehensive than earlier employment programs for ex-offenders, incorporating other transitional services and reentry support though maintaining a primary focus on job placement (Buck, 2000). The effects of these comprehensive, employment-focused programs on ex-offenders' employment and recidivism rates are not yet known; several well-designed evaluations are under way.

Marriage and Family Support Programs

For the general population, research has documented the benefits of marriage for adults and their children (see Chapter 2; Waite and Gallagher, 2000; Lerman, 2002). A recent study concluded that marriage is a "potentially transformative institution that may assist in promoting desistance from criminal behavior" (Sampson et al., 2006, p. 500). Thus, it makes sense to ask whether former prisoners would benefit from marriage and family support programs.

Most people in prisons are men, and most of them are fathers. A majority of state and federal male prisoners have at least one child under 18, on average 8 years old (Mumola, 2000). About one-third of the fathers lived with their children just before arrest, and most also lived with the child's mother. Some who did not live with their children saw them regularly and contributed to their upbringing (Hairston, 2002). Over one-half of incarcerated parents have been married, and about 23 percent are married when they are in prison (Mumola, 2000).

In addition to the role of marriage in contributing to desistance, a significant body of research shows positive effects of family support on a variety of reentry outcomes. Greater contact with family during incarceration (by mail, phone, or in-person visits) is associated with lower recidivism rates (Adams and Fischer, 1976; Glaser, 1969; Hairston, 2002). Prisoners with close family ties have lower recidivism rates than those without such attachments (La Vigne et al., 2004; Sullivan et al., 2002). Strong family attachments may keep ex-offenders away from peers who encourage criminal behavior (Warr, 1998). Emotional and financial family support is associ-

---

[2]The reason for these differences is not clear, but is probably due to a slightly different mix of studies. In addition, Visher and her colleagues included only randomized clinical trials in their analysis, while Amos and his colleagues included matched designs.

ated with better employment and the avoidance of illegal substance use (La Vigne et al., 2004; Visher et al. 2003; Nelson et al., 1999; Sullivan et al., 2002). Fathers who report strong attachments to their children have higher employment and lower depression rates after release (Visher et al., 2007). Family support is associated with better results concerning depression and prosocial identity (Ekland-Olson et al., 1983; Uggen, Manza, and Behrens, 2004; Laub and Sampson, 2003).

Prison-based programs generally offer parenting education, counseling and support groups, and services to facilitate visitation. Community-based programs usually include counseling, mentoring, assistance with family reunification and rebuilding, continuing parenting education, and family support groups. However, support services specifically focused on marriage and family for prisoners and former prisoners are limited and generally have not directly addressed nonmarital couple relationships. Some programs provide family strengthening services that may affect couples, but indirectly, by attempting to help fathers to be less of a burden to their families, to strengthen the father-child bond, and to avoid behaviors that stress relationships. Other programs focus on family relationships more generally. Programs funded as part of the federal Serious and Violent Offender Reentry Initiative (SVORI) offer general family strengthening services, but only 8 of the 50 adult programs ranked it as one of their top three priorities (see http://www.svori-evaluation.org [accessed June 2007]).

Unfortunately, few intervention studies have examined the role of marriage and family support programs in desistance. An exception is La Bodega de Familia, a well-known family-focused reentry program for former prisoners developed in New York City. The program uses comprehensive family case management as a mechanism for working with releasees and people on probation, families, and the community to create a web of support. Comprehensive family case management uses a strengths-based, client-driven approach to help clients and family members navigate service delivery systems and agencies to access treatment and services, maintain employment, tap existing networks for support, and create long-term family well-being and community safety (Shapiro, 2003). An evaluation of the program demonstrated that focusing on returning former prisoners together with their families, and emphasizing the strengths of each unit in addition to addressing the deficits, successfully decreased illegal drug use without additional treatment, reduced new arrests, and increased overall physical and mental health (Sullivan et al., 2002). One negative outcome was that the clients (former prisoners and their families) reported increased conflict in their family relationships.

In 2006 the Department of Health and Human Services initiated a demonstration program designed to promote two-parent families and marriage, with a special focus on incarcerated fathers. Ten sites were chosen for an in-depth process and outcome evaluation; where possible, couples will be randomly assigned to the demonstration program or another set of services (see http://www.acf.hhs.gov/programs/ofa/hmabstracts/summary.htm [accessed March 2006]). When the evaluation is completed, this highly innovative program may offer insights into the relationship between marriage-strengthening programs and successful reentry of releasees. However, given the research on the important role of nonmarital family support after release, demonstration programs are also needed to identify the types of programs and services that would be most effective in promoting desistance.

Behavior Management

The desistance literature points to individual motivation to change as a key correlate of reduced offending (Maruna, 2001; Laub and Sampson, 2001). Behavior management therapies in correctional programming seek to help individuals understand the basis for their negative behavior and correct their faulty perceptions of themselves, their environment, or both. These therapies provide individuals with skills they can use to monitor their thoughts and correct their behaviors in daily situations, ultimately leading to significant changes in behavior. Behavior management is an umbrella approach that includes contingency management (relapse prevention), social learning, and moral reasoning techniques. In relapse prevention, clients are guided to evaluate situations that may lead to a relapse of illegal behavior and then plan for how to either avoid or cope with them effectively.

The most widely recognized behavior management approach to change is cognitive-behavioral therapy or treatment. In the criminal justice field, it is a problem-focused method designed to help people identify the dysfunctional beliefs, thoughts, and patterns of behavior that contribute to their problems and provide them with the skills they need to modify those behaviors, prevent relapse into those behaviors, and maintain successful behavior (Taxman, 2006). This approach also addresses individuals' readiness and motivation to change by engaging them in self-assessment and the development of treatment goals. The underlying theory of cognitive-behavioral treatment is that behavior is learned, and mechanisms for learning new behaviors must be in place in order for the environment to be part of the change process (Taxman, 2006). It combines two kinds of approaches—cognitive therapy and behavioral therapy.

Cognitive therapy concentrates on thoughts, assumptions, and beliefs. Through cognitive therapy, individuals are encouraged to recognize and change faulty or maladaptive thinking patterns that lead to negative behavior. Cognitive therapy enables individuals to gain control over inappropriate repetitive thoughts that often feed or trigger various presenting problems

(Beck, 1995). Behavior therapy concentrates on external factors, addressing the specific actions and environments that either change or maintain behaviors (Skinner, 1974; Bandura, 1977). For instance, people who are trying to stop smoking are often encouraged to change their routine habits: instead of having their daily coffee when waking—which may trigger the urge to have a cigarette—they are encouraged to take a morning walk. Replacing negative behaviors with positive behaviors is a well-known strategy to help change behaviors, particularly when the new behavior is reinforced.

Cognitive-behavioral approaches have often been used in correctional programs that target substance use and its associated problems. The theory is that substance use is a learned behavior that is initiated and maintained in the context of environmental factors (Waldron and Kaminer, 2004). Programs built on this premise concentrate on helping people anticipate and avoid high-risk situations as a means to facilitate abstinence. Techniques used to facilitate change include identifying the circumstances surrounding use, learning strategies to manage urges and cravings, and remembering to engage in positive behaviors (Kaminer, 2004).

The combination of cognitive therapy and behavioral therapy has been successful, especially among young people, in forestalling the onset, ameliorating the severity, and diverting the long-term consequences of behaviors associated with delinquency, crime, and violence. Research consistently shows that cognitive-behavioral therapy is associated with significant and clinically meaningful positive changes, particularly when therapy is provided by experienced practitioners (Landenberger and Lipsey, 2006; Waldron and Kaminer, 2004). Four problem behaviors have been particularly amenable to change with this approach: (1) violence and criminality, (2) substance use and abuse, (3) teenage pregnancy and risky sexual behaviors, and (4) school failure. Cognitive-behavioral therapy has been successfully applied across settings (e.g., schools, support groups, prisons, treatment agencies, community-based organizations, and churches) and across ages and roles (e.g., students, parents, and teachers). It has also been shown to be relevant to people with differing abilities and from diverse backgrounds.

Meta-analyses of programs designed for criminal offenders have shown cognitive-behavioral programs to be very effective in reducing recidivism rates, most notably among higher risk, hard-to-reach offenders (Little, 2005; Lipsey et al., 2001; Landenberger and Lipsey, 2006).[3] On average, the therapy reduced the recidivism rates of a general offender population by 27 percent. Interestingly, in a study of prisoners who received cognitive-behavioral treatment either through participation in programs with high-quality implementation (e.g., research and demonstration projects) or in

---

[3]The Landenberger and Lipsky (2006) meta-analysis is particularly notable because it included only studies that used random control designs.

routine correctional practice, those in the former group experienced higher reductions in recidivism rates after release (49% on average) than the latter group (11% on average). The largest effects on recidivism were seen for higher risk offenders who received treatment from providers with at least moderate training in cognitive-behavioral therapy and as part of research and demonstration projects. For this group, recidivism rates were reduced by nearly 60 percent. Overall, however, Landenberger and Lipsey (2006) found no difference in the effectiveness of various "brand name" programs of cognitive-behavioral therapy in comparison with generic forms of the therapy.

In their latest review of the evidence from 291 rigorous evaluations of adult corrections programs throughout the United States and other English-speaking countries, Aos et al. (2006) found that programs for the general offender population that use cognitive-behavioral treatment significantly reduced recidivism by an average of 8.2 percent compared with treatment as usual.[4] That is, without the cognitive behavioral approach 49 percent of offenders will recidivate, and with cognitive behavioral treatment, 45 percent of offenders will recidivate, a reduction of 8.2 percent in the recidivism rate. Prison-based drug treatment programs that use cognitive-behavioral approaches have been found to reduce recidivism by nearly 7 percent (Aos et al., 2006, Exhibit 1). Finally, cognitive-behavioral treatment programs have also been shown to be cost-effective, yielding $2.54 to $11.48 for every program dollar invested in comparison with punishment-oriented interventions, which have yielded returns of only 50 to 75 cents for every program dollar (Aos et al., 2001).

Treatment for Drug-Involved Offenders

Illegal drugs are related to crime in multiple ways, and the connection between drug use and crime has been well established in the research literature. According to the Bureau of Justice Statistics (1998), 31 percent of crime victims reported that their assailants were under the influence of drugs or alcohol. In 2005 approximately 20 percent of state prison inmates and 55 percent of federal prison inmates were incarcerated for a drug related offense, and among state prisoners, three-fourths had some type of involvement with drug or alcohol abuse prior to their incarceration.

Substance use among former prisoners presents significant challenges to their reentry. Only 15 percent of offenders involved with drugs and alcohol abuse received treatment in prison (Karburg and James, 2005). Serious drug use problems—involving daily or weekly use—likely affects about

---

[4] As with the other meta-analysis, there were no significant differences in outcome between the "brand name" and generic forms of treatment.

one-third to one-half of all drug-abusing offenders. Forty-one percent of men released from Maryland prisons and returning to Baltimore reported using heroin daily in the 6 months before their incarceration; about 33 percent of men released from Illinois prisons reported weekly illicit drug use before incarceration (Visher et al., 2004; Visher et al., 2003). Because chronic drug abuse alters the brain chemistry in people addicted to heroin, cocaine, and even nicotine, they are at higher risk of relapse to use even after long periods of abstinence (National Institute on Drug Abuse, 2006). In addition, releasees who are substance users also have high rates of other mental health problems, so they may need integrated drug and psychiatric treatment (Compton et al., 2003). Such treatment may need to be relatively prolonged, because research has shown that multiple episodes of treatment may be required to help substance users maintain abstinence over time (National Institute on Drug Abuse, 2006).

A comprehensive assessment is the first step in developing a treatment regimen, and tailoring individualized services is an important component of drug abuse treatment for criminal justice populations (National Institute on Drug Abuse, 2006). The three primary treatment approaches for drug-abusing offenders are therapeutic communities, outpatient treatment, and "12-step" programs. Therapeutic communities are intensive programs that typically have stand-alone custodial units and use a hierarchical model with treatment stages that reflect increased levels of personal and social responsibility. Outpatient treatment involves counseling by certified drug treatment specialists and often includes pharmacotherapy. And 12-step programs are organized by peers, such as Alcoholics Anonymous (AA) and Narcotics Anonymous (NA).

It is widely believed that in-prison drug treatment for offenders leads to reductions in drug use and subsequent criminal behavior and to better outcomes in other areas, such as employment. However, there are few rigorous evaluations of in-prison drug treatment programs. Evaluations of the three most well-known model programs—Key/Crest (Delaware), the Amity therapeutic prison (California), and Kyle New Vision (Texas)—suffer from several methodological shortcomings, including noncomparable treatment and control groups, inadequate controls for selection bias, and poor outcome measures (Pearson and Lipton, 1999; Gaes et al., 1999). This lack of high-quality evaluations is especially troubling in light of congressional appropriations of more than $450 million to states in the last decade to establish residential substance abuse treatment programs in correctional institutions.

Unfortunately, even for the small group of individuals who have access to and take advantage of treatment programs in prison, available evidence suggests that fewer continue to receive such community-based treatment after release (Winterfield and Castro, 2005). In an analysis that examined the extent to which correctional treatment was matched to individual needs, a recent study of prisoners with drug problems found that only 58 percent of those who either had objective indicators of serious drug use or indicated a need for drug treatment received in-prison drug treatment (including Alcoholics Anonymous or Narcotics Anonymous) (Winterfield and Castro, 2005).

A recent meta-analysis of correctional programs concluded that drug-treatment programs reduce recidivism: the reduction is about 5 percent for releasees who received only in-prison treatment and 12 percent for releasees who received both in-prison and community treatment (Aos et al., 2006). An earlier study showed that some offenders may benefit from diversion into treatment, but others may require intensive monitoring with the threat of criminal justice sanctions (Marlowe, 2003).

Offenders who complete prison-based treatment and continue with treatment in the community have the best outcomes (National Institute on Drug Abuse, 2006; Gaes et al., 1999; Harrison and Beck, 2006). Continuing drug abuse treatment in the community is believed to be necessary to help new releasees deal with problems that only become salient at reentry, such as learning to handle situations that could lead to relapse, learning how to live drug free, and developing a drug-free peer support network. Moreover, better outcomes are also associated with treatment that lasts longer than 90 days, and studies have shown that legal pressure can improve retention rates (National Institute on Drug Abuse, 2006).

Increasingly, medications are an important part of treatment for serious drug abusers with long histories; those medications include methadone, buprenorphine, topiramate, and naltrexone (National Institute on Drug Abuse, 2006; Witten, 2006). Although these medications may not be appropriate for all drug-using offenders, the criminal justice system has been slow to embrace these approaches; and most parolees and other ex-offenders who are under criminal justice supervision in the community are not offered this type of treatment.[5] Yet postrelease monitoring of drug use through urinalysis or other objective methods, as part of criminal justice supervision, has been found to reduce both relapses of drug use and criminal behavior (Taxman, 2006). Ongoing coordination between treatment providers and courts or supervision officers is required to address the needs of the drug-abusing releasees (Marlowe, 2003), but collaboration and communication between the treatment and community criminal justice supervision systems have been limited to date.

In summary, although sustained abstinence is associated with substantial reductions in crime (perhaps 50 percent or more), only a small percentage of drug-abusing offenders receive appropriate treatment for the length

---

[5] A few adult drug courts do include medication-based treatment (see below and Chapter 5).

of time necessary to achieve these outcomes (Harrell and Roman, 2001; Marlowe, 2003). Best practice would call for better targeted in-prison treatment for substance-using offenders, better coordination between in-prison and postrelease treatment providers, and better joint community case management between the criminal justice system and community treatment providers.

REENTRY PROGRAMMING

In addition to the effects of improved access to appropriate drug treatment programs, jobs and job training, and family support services, reentry programming shows promise in addressing issues and situations that may cause offenders to cycle in and out of prison. Reentry services and programs for releasees focus on immediate needs, such as developing an individualized plan for the first few weeks and months after release; working with a case manager in the community; meeting housing, physical health, and mental health needs; and providing mentoring programs for support.

Planning Prior to Release

Released prisoners face enormous challenges, from finding jobs and housing to staying sober to avoiding high-risk persons and places. One key to successful reentry is identifying the challenges prior to release and developing tailored reentry plans that identify appropriate services. Research emphasizes the importance of conducting detailed needs assessments shortly before release and periodically after release to develop appropriate individualized services. Because it is widely agreed that not every offender needs the same level and type of service and sanction and that offenders differ on their likelihood to reoffend once released back into the community (Andrews and Bonta, 1998; Weibush, McNulty, and Le, 2000; Weibush et al., 2005), such assessments are the foundation for an individualized reentry plan.

An individualized reentry plan not only specifies what services and supervision level are appropriate for each releasee, but also specifies what documents, medications, or other immediate transition preparation a releasee may need. An individualized plan for a releasee then connects to individualized and unified case planning and management. The ideal case management approach incorporates a family and social network perspective, a mix of surveillance and services that takes account of a releasee's risk and protective factors, and realistic and enforceable release conditions that are connected with graduated incentives and consequences (i.e., graduated responses, discussed in Chapter 3). It also relies on community service providers and resources and other supportive community organizations

(Jenkins, Griswold, and Gillespie, 1993; see http://nicic.org/Library/011018 [accessed September 2007]). The importance of developing these reentry plans to enable people to succeed once they have been released has been described by Petersilia (2003) and Healy (1999). Unfortunately, such individualized reentry plans are not yet standard operating practice prior to release, largely because of lack of resources to fund staff to prepare them.

Early Failure and Its Consequences

When they leave prison, releasees most immediately need transitional services. Transitional services include photo identifications, appropriate clothes, housing, access to transportation, and, if they are eligible, getting signed up for public assistance. Unfortunately, these kinds of immediate needs are often not addressed before release, and it falls to family and friends to help arrange them for new releasees. In fact, most postrelease programs are not available to releasees in the first few days after release. This lack of immediately available services has been shown in recent research to have serious consequences: releasees are at high risk of dying or being rearrested within the first few days and weeks after release.

In a recent special article for the *New England Journal of Medicine*, Binswanger and colleagues (2007) found that former prison inmates were at relatively high risk of death after release, particularly during the first 2 weeks. The article reports on a retrospective cohort study of all inmates released from the Washington State Department of Corrections from July 1999 through December 2003. The risk of death during the first 2 weeks after release, adjusted for age, sex, and race, was 12.7 times that of other state residents. The leading causes of death for former inmates were drug overdose, cardiovascular disease, homicide, and suicide, which are different from the leading causes of death in the state's general population and in the prison population.[6]

It has been well established that a large proportion of parolees who return to prison fail in the first weeks and months after their release (Maltz, 1984; Schmidt and Witte, 1988; Ezell, 2007; Haapanen et al., 2007). In a recent analysis, Rosenfeld and colleagues, using data from the Bureau of Justice Statistics, calculated arrest probabilities by month for each of the 36 months postrelease for a sample of 243,334 released prisoners in 13 states. Roughly two-thirds of prison releasees are arrested at least once during this

---

[6]The study found that of 30,237 released inmates, 443 died during an average follow-up period of 1.9 years. The overall mortality rate was 777 deaths per 100,000 person-years. The adjusted risk of death among former inmates was 3.5 times that for other state residents. During the first 2 weeks after release, the risk of death among former inmates was 12.7 times that for other state residents, with a markedly elevated relative risk of death from drug overdose, a shocking 129 times that of the general population.

3-year postrelease period (Langan and Levin, 2002). In one analysis, the researchers assumed that the entire sample was eligible for arrest in any given month. A second analysis adjusts that probability by subtracting out persons who were in jail, in prison, or dead during the month and therefore not eligible for arrest. In both cases, the probability of arrest declines with months out of prison: that probability during the first month out of prison is roughly double that during the 15th month, and it then stabilizes through the end of the 3-year period (see Figure 4-1).

The probability of arrest after release from prison differs by type of crime. Prison releasees arrested for property or drug offenses are more likely to be arrested early in the postrelease period than those arrested for violent offenses. This pattern is illustrated in Figure 4-2, which shows the probability of arrest for releases arrested for property, drug, and violent crimes. The arrest probabilities have been adjusted for time off the street. Although risk for arrest declines over time for all three crime types, a much steeper decline occurs for property and drug offenders, whose arrest risk drops by nearly 50 percent between the 1st and 15th month after release; for violent offenders, the decline is only about 20 percent from the 1st to the 15th month out of prison. Given these data, it is difficult to overstate the importance for parolees and their communities of access to

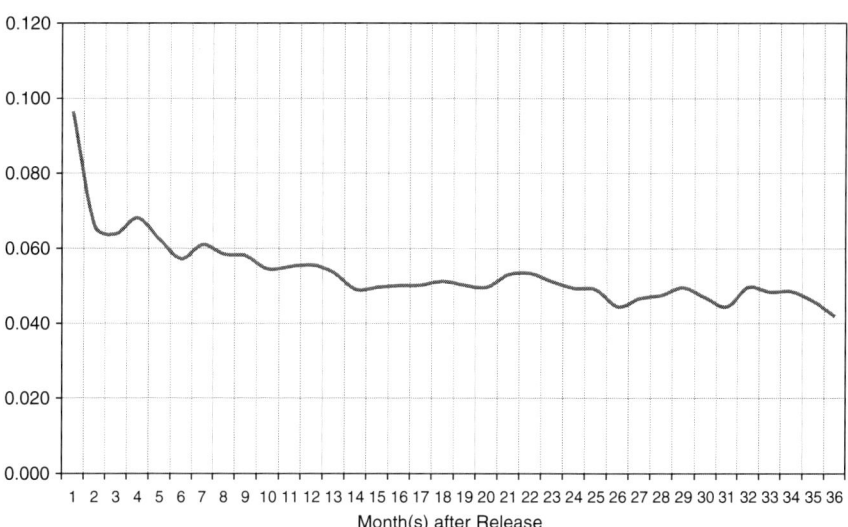

FIGURE 4-1 Probability of arrest for a new crime after release from prison.
NOTE: Probabilities adjusted for time off the street.
SOURCE: Richard Rosenfeld, personal communication, January 10, 2007.

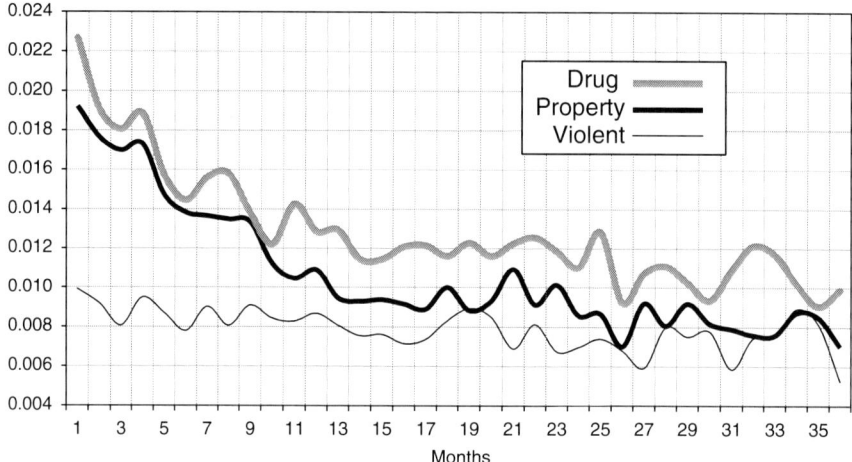

FIGURE 4-2 Probability of arrest for a violent, property, or drug crime 36 months after release from prison.
NOTE: Probabilities adjusted for time off the street.
SOURCE: The analysis for this figure was conducted by Rosenfeld et al. (2005).

both supportive and transitional reentry services in those first days, weeks, and months out of prison.

Housing Needs and Barriers

Securing housing is perhaps the most immediate challenge facing prisoners after release. Although most new releasees can count on family or friends to provide housing, those who cannot have very limited housing options. The situation is often complicated by a host of factors: the scarcity of affordable and available housing in many cities, legal barriers, preconceptions that restrict tenancy for this population, and local eligibility requirements for federally subsidized housing that may exclude many releasees, such as those who were convicted of drug offenses. Housing eligibility restrictions on ex-offenders are a critical public policy factor in planning reentry. Such restrictions and other barriers may lead to a concentration of releasees in low-rent, distressed neighborhoods, environs that are hardly conducive to successful reintegration.

Released prisoners who do not have stable housing arrangements are more likely to return to prison (Metraux and Culhane, 2004). This finding suggests that the obstacles to securing both temporary and permanent housing warrant the attention of policy makers, practitioners, and researchers. Supportive housing programs—such as the Oxford House model, originally conceived as a drug and alcohol addiction recovery program for substance users, and halfway houses that include on-site services (see Roman and Travis, 2004)—could be an option for former prisoners, but they have not been implemented on a wide scale (Jason et al., 2006).[7] Mutual-help models like Oxford House are particularly effective at providing positive peer networks and may be an appropriate model for postrelease housing for former prisoners (Olson et al., 2005).

Peer Support and Individualized Services

More generally, greater peer support from other formerly incarcerated people is associated with less recidivism (Broome et al., 1996). In fact, the presence of other recovering peers has been shown to be more effective in achieving desistance than the involvement of clinical staff or correctional officers alone (Wexler, 1995). The most rigorous research study on this question was a randomized trial of an Oxford House program that tracked more than 90 percent of the participants, (substance abusers, often with criminal records) for 2 years: it found 50 percent less recidivism, among Oxford House residents than among a control group. Employment at the 2-year follow-up was also significantly higher among Oxford House participants (Jason et al., 2006).

Another reentry programming approach is a package of individualized services for new releasees that has been referred to as "wraparound" service delivery. As the name suggests, it involves a comprehensive array of individualized services and support networks that are wrapped around clients, rather than presenting them only with set, inflexible treatment programs (Walker and Bruns, 2003). In the wraparound model, treatment services are usually provided by multiple agencies working together as part of a collaborative interagency agreement, and each new releasee's service plan is developed and managed by an interdisciplinary team that includes a caseworker, family members and community residents, and several social services and mental health professionals.

Wraparound interventions are different from traditional case management programs, which simply provide individuals with one caseworker

---

[7]Researchers at DePaul University have been actively investigating this model for over 10 years and have produced dozens of manuscripts on its advantages; see, for example, Davis et al. (2006). One of the researchers, Dr. Brad Olson, is an adviser to the Safer Foundation's programs. The mission of the foundation as posted on its website is to reduce recidivism by supporting, through a full spectrum of services: the efforts of offenders to become productive, law-abiding members of the community (see http://www.saferfoundation.org/viewpage.asp?id=4 [accessed August 2007].

whose job is to guide them through the existing social services and try to ensure that they receive appropriate services. Wraparound programs feature several basic elements, including the collaborative team described above; interagency agreements; care-case coordinators to supervise diverse cases and treatment management; a family orientation; and a unified plan of service delivery. Wraparound approaches also emphasize the importance of recruiting committed staff and creating programs that are culturally competent and "strengths based" (see below) (Barton, 2006; Walker and Bruns, 2006). Wraparound programs with basic elements have become increasingly popular since the model was introduced in the 1980s.

Strengths-based approaches attempt to rebalance the traditional focus on an individual's problems, pathologies, and deficits, which can be demeaning and unproductive; instead, they focus on resilience, positive psychology, empowerment theories, and brief therapeutic approaches, such as solution-focused work and assessment and practices to capitalize on individual strengths (DeJong and Berg, 2002; Burnett and Maruna, 2004; Taxman, 2006). This approach has been found to work with families, substance abusers, and people with mental health problems, especially juvenile offenders (Early and GlenMaye, 2000; Rapp-Paglicchi and Roberts, 2004). The focus is on assessing and leveraging client capabilities, talents, and resources to support change and solve problems from a positive perspective. Belief in a client's strength and focusing on his or her ability to change can foster motivation rather than resistance (Clark and Lee, 2005).

AVAILABLE SERVICES AND THEIR EFFECTS

Physical Health Services

The incarcerated population in the United States is composed mostly of poor, urban, and undereducated people who have a high prevalence of health problems. They not only have higher rates of substance abuse and violence than the general population, but they also suffer high rates of physical health problems. Their generally riskier life-styles increase the prevalence of infectious diseases, such as HIV/AIDS, tuberculosis, sexually transmitted diseases, and hepatitis (see Brewer, 2001). In addition to infectious disease, their relatively higher rates of lack of access to health care, combined with poverty, substandard nutrition, and poor housing or homelessness contribute to increased risk for such chronic conditions as hypertension, cardiovascular disease, skin conditions, gastrointestinal disease, diabetes, and asthma.

The effects of physical health problems on reentry for releasees has received some attention (Travis, 2005), but the effects have not been carefully or widely studied. One preliminary study suggests that releasees with medical problems are more likely to experience difficulties in reentry than those without such problems (Visher and Mallik-Kane, 2007).

In recent years, legal mandates have required correctional systems to provide physical and mental health care to prisoners. And with an increase in the accreditation of correctional health care provision (by the American Correctional Association and the National Commission on Correctional Health Care), the quality of such care has come under greater scrutiny.

The most innovative approach to the provision of reentry-focused health care is a program developed at the Hampden County Correctional Center in Massachusetts. Neighborhood health centers and the institution developed a collaboration that fostered both greater in-prison provision of quality health care services and more consistent linkages to needed services after a prisoner's release. Health care providers and social service professionals work together as part of a team from each health center: a case manager with expertise in the social service needs of inmates and releasees strongly complements the health care delivered by physicians and nurses. The comprehensive approach ensures that inmates receive high-quality care and reduces the risks to good health after release (i.e., homelessness, substance abuse relapse, and lack of health insurance). An evaluation of the Hampden County program funded by the National Institute of Justice (Hammett et al., 2004) found that participants reported significantly better overall health, more interaction with community health care providers, and less frequent use of alcohol and hard drugs in the 6 months after release in comparison with the period before incarceration. However, an analysis of criminal history records revealed no relationship between recidivism and participation in the program. Moreover, there was no comparison group in this study. Replications of this program are being funded by the Robert Wood Johnson Foundation in nine sites, and an evaluation is planned.

Mental Health Services

The deinstitutionalization of mentally ill people that occurred during the 1960s and early 1970s rested on several assumptions. A key one was that people with mental illness could find and easily access community mental health services. Unfortunately, this assumption has not proved true. The lack of community facilities for mentally ill people has had the unintended consequence of making the criminal justice system the primary public response to problem behaviors associated with severe mental illness. Among prisoners, the rates of mental illness are two to four times higher than among the general population (Lurigio, 2001). In a 1998 survey, approximately 16 percent of those in state prisons, local jails, or on probation said they either had a mental condition or had stayed overnight in a mental hospital, unit, or treatment program (Ditton, 1999), about twice as high as estimates of mental illness from the National Survey on Drug Use and Health among the general population (see http://www.oas.samhsa.gov/nhsda.htm [accessed June 2007]). A more recent study reports that about one-half of state and federal prison inmates have a mental health problem, based on self-reports of treatment or diagnosis during the previous 12 months or on symptoms classified by interviewers using standard criteria (James and Glaze, 2006). Only about one-third of state prison inmates and one-quarter of federal inmates with a mental health problem reported having received mental health treatment since admission to prison.

Until the early 1990s, most mentally ill defendants could expect to be processed by the criminal justice system in the same manner as defendants without mental illness. In the past 10–15 years, however, more innovative approaches have been initiated. Two federal funding initiatives—the targeted capacity expansion diversion program of the Substance Abuse and Mental Health Services Administration and the mental health courts grant program of the Bureau of Justice Assistance—have provided resources for new approaches for mentally ill offenders.

In 1992, a national survey of jail diversion programs estimated that only about 52 jails had some kind of diversion program for offenders with mental illness (Monahan and Steadman, 1994); by 2003, the number had increased to 294 (U.S. Department of Health and Human Services, 2004). The approaches are not uniform. They include a variety of interventions that facilitate the provision of services to offenders in order to speed their release from incarceration. The overriding purpose of diversion programs is to provide services and reduce the length of incarceration; some also attempt to reduce or dismiss the charges brought against offenders. A cross-site evaluation of nine jail diversion programs found that, in general, the programs decreased the number of days spent incarcerated, thereby reducing criminal justice costs, and also reduced rearrests among participants (U.S. Department of Health and Human Services, 2004).

A different approach for mentally ill offenders is mental health courts, a judicially managed program that relies on therapeutic jurisprudence (modeled after drug courts), in which the primary focus is on reduction or dismissal of the charges when a specified treatment regimen is successfully completed. In the late 1990s, only a few such courts accepted cases; since then, some 70 others have been established or are in planning stages. In 2000, the Mental Health Courts Grant Program was created by the America's Law Enforcement and Mental Health Project Act. The program is managed by the Bureau of Justice Assistance, which provided grants to 37 courts in 2002 and 2003. The agency also funded technical assistance for all existing courts through 2006. As of July 2006, there were 113 mental health courts that responded to a survey conducted by the National Alliance for the Mentally Ill, the National GAINS Center for People with Co-Occurring

Disorders in the Justice System, the TAPA Center for Jail Diversion, and the Council of State Governments.[8] Under a court's authority, defendants undergo regular therapy sessions and their medication is often monitored, sometimes allowing them to avoid prison time. Because of the newness of these courts, little is known about their effectiveness or whether the effects for parolees may differ from those for other criminal justice populations. Current research examining mental health courts is under way.

Mentoring Programs

Mentoring programs have a long history in delinquency prevention, and evaluation studies show positive effects for at-risk and delinquent youth (see Branch and Tierney, 2000; Herrera et al., 2000). The goal of mentoring is to support the development of prosocial life-styles, thereby reducing an individual's exposure to or the temptations of risky and problem behaviors.

Certain elements are essential to effective mentoring programs, including a high level of contact between mentor and mentee and a relationship that defines the mentor as a trusted adviser and supporter rather than an authority figure. There are several factors that serve as prerequisites for successful mentoring programs, including: (1) volunteer screening to eliminate inappropriate mentors, (2) communication and limit-setting training for mentors, (3) procedures that take account of mentors' and mentees' preferences, and (4) intensive supervision and support of each match (Center for Substance Abuse Prevention, 2000).

An analysis (Jolliffe and Farrington, 2007) of 18 studies in the United States and the United Kingdom on the impact of mentoring on ex-offenders and recidivism found the following:

- Of 18 studies, 7 showed that mentoring of ex-offenders had a statistically positive effect.
- Subsequent offending was reduced by 4 to 11 percent.
- The methodologically superior studies did not show a significant reduction in reoffending.
- Programs that reduced recidivism used more frequent and longer mentoring sessions: once or more per week and 5 hours or more per session.

---

[8]For the purpose of the survey, mental health courts were defined as adult criminal courts that (1) had a separate docket dedicated to persons with mental illnesses; (2) diverted criminal defendants from jail into treatment programs; and (3) monitored the defendants during treatment and had the ability to impose criminal sanctions for failures to comply with program requirements.

- Mentoring was only successful in reducing recidivism when included in a menu of interventions.
- The benefits of mentoring did not appear to persist after mentoring ended.

Maruna (2001) has argued that the benefits of the mentoring process are often greater for the mentor than for the mentee (see also Cressy's (1955) notion of "reflexive reformation").

Adult mentoring programs for former prisoners are being studied in the context of the DOL's program, Ready4Work (R4W) Program, which also has a strong faith-based component. The mentors and coaches are drawn from the community, especially faith-based organizations. Focus groups indicate that the clients (potential mentees) want mentoring, and they express a particular preference for mentors who have had a prisoner/reentry experience. Both individual and group mentoring models are being implemented.[9] Once they are involved in the program, mentees continue to want mentoring, and they also want to become mentors themselves, participating as both a mentor and a mentee. Several Ready4Work participants have "graduated" and become mentors.

A preliminary report provides examples of mentoring in the R4W sites that appear promising (Jucovy, 2006). An evaluation of the program now under way will examine the frequency and duration of participation in the mentoring aspects of R4W as it relates to a releasee's successful reentry. The DOL has included mentoring as a key component in its new Prisoner Reentry Initiative, again with an emphasis on faith-based organizations as the source of the mentors.

Despite the variety and promising prospects of the approaches just described, community services currently available for new releasees may not be meeting their needs. In a survey of men released from state prison to Chicago, 48 percent said that they had used some services in the 2 months since release (MacKenzie, 2006; La Vigne and Cowan, 2005; Giordano et al., 2002), but when asked what services were most useful, 17 percent said that none of them was useful. When asked "what would be most helpful right now" (6 months postrelease), 64 percent mentioned a job or job training, 53 percent mentioned financial support, 24 percent mentioned education, 38 percent mentioned housing, and 41 percent mentioned health insurance (La Vigne et al., 2006).

Nonetheless, in community corrections, there is a research base suggesting what works at the individual offender level. The effects of a variety of programs for those returning to communities have been examined in com-

---

[9]Preliminary evidence suggests that group mentoring may not be as powerful as traditional mentoring (Herrera et al., 2002), although it may be a less costly alternative.

prehensive reviews of evaluations. One showed that parolees who stayed in halfway houses after release committed less severe and less frequent crimes (Seiter and Kadela, 2003). A second review showed that those intensive supervision programs with a strong treatment component had a sizable effect on recidivism (Aos et al., 2006). A third review concluded that human service-oriented programs are much more effective than those based on a control or deterrent philosophy. All of the strategies identified as effective by MacKenzie (2006) target dynamic criminogenic factors, are skill oriented, are based on cognitive-behavioral models, and treat multiple offender deficits simultaneously in particular, there is growing consensus that practices focusing on individual-level change, including cognitive change, education, and drug treatment, are likely to be more effective than other strategies, such as programs that only increase opportunities for work, reunite families, or provide housing (MacKenzie, 2006; Andrews and Bonta, 2003). These conclusions are consistent with several large meta-analyses of the evaluation literature (Aos et al., 2006; Andrews et al., 1990; Lipsey, 1995; Lipsey and Cullen, 2007).

These findings seem to be somewhat at odds with the longitudinal research on desistance, which highlights the conditions that lead to law-abiding behavior, such as having a stable marriage and having strong ties to work (see Sampson and Laub, 1993; Laub and Sampson, 2003). However, it may be that programs associated with the desistance findings have had weak designs or implementation problems or that the evaluations have been flawed. Or it may be that individual-level change is a prerequisite for the conditions under which desistance takes hold. Or it may be that programs that target these conditions would be more successful if operated in close connection to individual change modalities.

Best Practices Design and Implementation Problems

The only evaluation of a contemporary prisoner reentry program to use a random assignment design, Project Greenlight in New York, demonstrates the implementation difficulties facing these programs (Wilson and Davis, 2006). Project Greenlight was developed by the Vera Institute of Justice on the basis of research and best practice models, and the institute believed it was creating an evidence-based reentry program. However, a thorough examination of the proposed model and its implementation revealed that the program modified best practices to fit institutional requirements, was delivered ineffectively, did not match individual needs to services, and failed to implement any postrelease continuation of services and support (Wilson and Davis, 2006; see also Visher, 2006; Marlowe, 2006).

The evaluation found that the program participants performed significantly worse than a control group on multiple measures of recidivism after

1 year, a finding that the evaluators attribute to a combination of implementation difficulties, program design, and a mismatch between participant needs and program content. In response to the evaluation report, Marlowe (2006) argues that the evidence base for the program was flawed from the beginning, with weak designs and unproven, unstandardized interventions. Edward Rhine of the Ohio Department of Rehabilitation and Correction- and colleagues (2006) are more optimistic about reentry programming in general, and point out that Project Greenlight was not notably different from other failed reentry programs and that the treatment was not delivered appropriately (see also Wilson and Davis, 2006; Visher, 2006; Marlowe, 2006).

CONCLUSIONS

This review of programs and services for former prisoners suggests three main conclusions regarding their effectiveness in reducing recidivism and problem behaviors. First, there is scientific evidence that several programs and approaches reduce violations of community supervision requirements, arrests for new crimes, and drug use. They include cognitive-behavioral therapeutic approaches and frequent testing for drug use, coupled with treatment. Mentoring programs and comprehensive multiservice employment initiatives show promise but require further, more rigorous research.

Second, inadequate implementation of program principles and procedures appears to be a significant obstacle in the way of being able to determine program effectiveness or finding out whether a program might have benefits for participants.

Third, a major limitation of current program evaluation results is the failure to account fully for self-selection bias. Random assignment of persons to treatment and control conditions remains rare in research on the reentry process. Greater use of experimental designs, when such designs are feasible, is essential for drawing valid conclusions about reentry program effectiveness. When such designs are not feasible, greater attention should be paid to the selection of comparison groups and statistical adjustments for existing differences between program participants and nonparticipants. Although the field has moved beyond "nothing works" in assessments of program effects on reentry outcomes, it can identify with high confidence only a very few best practices for reducing recidivism and enhancing desistance among people leaving prison to return to local communities. More research, especially more experimental research, is needed to identify interventions that could significantly improve outcomes of community supervision for parolees (see Chapter 6).

5

Criminal Justice Institutions and Community Resources

ROLE OF THE COURTS

As policy makers struggle with the challenges of prisoner reentry, attention has increasingly focused on what role the courts might play. In the current allocation of responsibilities for prisoner reentry, courts traditionally play a marginal role. Usually a court's responsibility ends when a defendant is found or pleads guilty and is sentenced by the judge. Appellate courts may hear issues on appeal, but the trial judge's responsibility usually ends when the trial ends. Judges typically have no role in the broad array of activities that carry out the terms of the sentence, prepare the inmate for release, or transition the returning prisoner back to his status as a member of the community (Office of Justice Programs, 1999). However, in the last 15 years, courts have begun to play a more active role in overseeing the sentences they impose, and there is growing interest in a new form of jurisprudence whereby judges oversee "specialized" or "problem-solving" courts with the goal of assisting in offender rehabilitation.

Some seven years ago, *Court Review*, the official journal of the American Judges Association, devoted an entire special issue (Vol. 37, No. 1) to the theme of therapeutic jurisprudence, an interdisciplinary perspective that seeks to augment the law by bringing to it insights from psychology, criminology, social work, and related behavioral sciences. The special issue of *Court Review* is significant because it evidences a movement of therapeutic jurisprudence from an academic perspective to a tool for actually changing practice. The special issue was introduced by Judge William Schma (2000) in an article titled "Judging for the New Millennium." Applying a therapeutic jurisprudence perspective in practice, Judge Schma advocates that judges become active "problem-solvers" in their courtrooms.

Therapeutic jurisprudence has been most readily brought into play in judicial proceedings of specialized treatment-oriented courts, or "problem-solving courts." Therapeutic jurisprudence recognizes the reality that the legal system may not have the expertise to solve social and behavioral problems, but that courts can lead a multidisciplinary team to promote behavioral change.

The most mature example of the judiciary's involvement in specialized courts the involve offender rehabilitation is the drug court. First implemented in 1989, the growth of drug courts has been unprecedented: there are now more than 1,550 drug courts now operating in the United States (National Institute of Justice, 2006). In a drug court, judges use a case management approach to identify and coordinate local services that help offenders refrain from drug use. When violations of the drug court contract occur, the judge usually administers a predetermined set of graduated, parsimonious sanctions for violations.

Studies suggest that recidivism rates are lower for drug court participants (and have been reported to be as low as 4% for program graduates), although the recidivism statistics vary by the characteristics of the specific drug court and its target population (National Institute of Justice, 2006). Unfortunately, many of these studies are not empirically rigorous; therefore, it is uncertain whether the drug court alone was responsible for the low recidivism rates. Nonetheless, the evidence does show that the best adult drug courts are effective at reducing system costs, crime, and drug use (U.S. Government Accountability Office, 2005). Urban Institute researcher John Roman (2005, available: http://www.urban.org/publications/900803.html.) recently summarized the available evidence noting:

> There have been more than 100 research studies about adult drug courts and if you look at the best, most rigorous 25 of those, you probably come to the conclusion that drug courts reduce criminal offending by 15 to 20 percent. So this is not a panacea but represents a real reduction in offending levels.

Judge Cindy Lederman of the 11th Judicial Circuit Court in Florida noted at the workshop that the essential component needed in a reentry court is some sort of motivation for a litigant to change. For example, in dependency courts, where therapeutic jurisprudence concepts have always been used and are even part of the law, people's children can be taken away, and yet many defendants are not motivated to do what is necessary to get their children back. Providing incentives for releasees to change may require fundamental changes in the law and in judicial and criminal justice philosophy. For these models to work for the more than 600,000 people who are released from prisons and return to local communities each year, a fundamental change in the use of judicial resources will almost certainly be required. The question becomes one of cost effectiveness: Is it worth it? Are these problem-solving courts better, more effective, than traditional courts that function well?

REENTRY COURTS

Due to the perceived success of drug courts, judges have become more receptive to new problem-solving approaches to adjudication, and the drug court model has now been extended to domestic violence courts, family treatment courts for dependency proceedings, mental health courts, and DWI offenses (driving while intoxicated or, in some jurisdictions, driving under the influence) (for an overview, see Casey and Rottman, 2003).

Jeremy Travis[1] urged the application of the specialized court model to prisoner reentry in 2000. As with drug courts, Travis proposed that active judicial authority could be applied to a "reentry court" to provide graduated sanction and positive reinforcement and to marshal resources for offender support. Drug courts usually operate *prior* to a prison sentence (e.g., as a diversion program); reentry courts would operate *after* prison (Travis, 2000).

In his book, *But They All Come Back*, Travis (2005) noted several benefits to reentry courts, saying that they cut across organizational boundaries, making it more likely that offenders are held accountable and supported in their reentry attempts. Reentry courts can also involve family members, friends, and others in a reentry plan. He also noted that judges command the public's confidence while, in contrast, the parole system is held in low public esteem. Moreover, judges carry out their business in open courtrooms, not closed offices, so the public, former prisoners, and family members and others can benefit from the open articulation of reasons for a government decision.

Travis also believes that a judge is in a unique position, given the prestige of the office, to confer public and official validation on an offender's reform efforts. Public ceremonies are thought to be critical to long-term success (Maruna and LeBel, 2003). Ideally, the judge who originally sentenced a prisoner would be the same judge who serves as that person's reentry manager. Most importantly, reentry courts explicitly give recognition to the fact that an offender will come back to live in the community.

---

[1]Then a senior scholar in residence at the Urban Institute in Washington, D.C., he had formerly been director of the National Institute of Justice; he is now president of John Jay College of Criminal Justice.

The core elements of both a drug court and a reentry court are similar (Office of Justice Programs, 1999):

- *Assessment and planning*: Following assessment of inmates' needs, corrections officials—working in conjunction with the reentry court judge—establish linkages to social services, housing, job training and work opportunities to support successful reintegration.
- *Active oversight*: Reentry court clients are seen frequently, probably once a month, beginning right after release and continuing until the end of their parole.
- *Management of support services*: A case manager brokers an array of resources.
- *Accountability to the community*: A mechanism exists for incorporating community perspectives, such as a citizen advisory board.
- *Graduate and parsimonious sanctions*: A predetermined range of sanctions for violations of parole conditions would be swiftly, predictably, and universally applied.
- *Rewards for success*: Milestones in the reentry process trigger recognition and rewards through positive judicial reinforcement (for example, graduation ceremonies and early release from parole supervision).

Operationally, a reentry process would start at the time of release from prison, when a "contract" would be drawn up between the court and a parolee.[2] The contract would list the conditions the parolee must follow, and the parolee would be required to appear in court every month to demonstrate how well the contract is working. The court appearances need not be long; they are designed to remind the parolee of the conditions in the contract. If the judge determined that a parolee needs more help, she or he could quickly mobilize the necessary resources. If a parolee failed to abide by the contract, the judge could use a variety of intermediate sanctions to encourage compliance. At the end of the period of supervision, the judge would oversee a "graduation ceremony." These ceremonies are designed to celebrate the individual's successful reentry into the community. Petersilia (2003) also endorsed the reentry court model and suggested that it incorporate goal-oriented parole, where the length of time in a reentry court would be reduced as an offender met or exceeded court expectations.

In February 2000 the Office of Justice Programs began the Reentry Courts Initiative (OJP-RCI), designed to provide technical assistance to jurisdictions interested in developing reentry courts. Nine pilot sites were

---

[2] Although we limit the discussion to parolees, in principle released prisoners who are not on parole could also fall under the jurisdiction of a reentry court.

selected: California, Colorado, Delaware, Florida, Iowa, Kentucky, New York, Ohio, and West Virginia. The programs operated rather similarly except for their target populations (see http://www.ojp.usdoj.gov/reentry/ communities.html [accessed August 2007]):

- One of Iowa's programs focused on offenders with dual diagnoses of mental health and addiction problems), that is, the drug addiction disorder co-occurred with their mental health disorder.
- Delaware's Reentry Court focused on offenders who had served particularly long prison terms.
- The Kentucky programs focused on nonviolent drug offenders who had served a portion of their sentence in prison and were then released to an outpatient drug treatment program for 1 year (Hiller et al., 2002).
- Ohio's reentry court created an expanded presentence report for prison-bound defendants, which was translated into a reentry plan. The Ohio Department of Rehabilitation and Corrections then provided the program services indicated on the reentry plan, and a newly created court-based position of "reentry liaison" visited the prisoner once a month while they were in prison. When the prisoner was released, he or she was brought back to the sentencing judge at the time of release for aftercare services and supervision (Wilkinson and Bucholtz, 2003).

A process evaluation of the reentry court pilot projects was done early in the program (Lindquist et al., 2003). The authors found that most reentry courts did offer comprehensive services to their program participants, including substance abuse treatment, family counseling, employment and vocational assistance, and housing assistance. Judges who participated in the reentry courts continued to be supportive of the model, although numerous obstacles were identified with program implementation. The most common obstacle noted was the difficulty in finding employment and affordable housing for parolees. The researchers also noted difficulties in interagency cooperation, particularly among parole authorities, treatment providers, and the judiciary. The researchers urged an outcome evaluation of the reentry court model, but it was never carried out.

At present, reentry courts are largely experimental, and neither their impact nor their costs and benefits have been rigorously evaluated. A 4-year study of inmates returning to Allen County, Indiana, found significant cost savings from the reentry court programs, but the offenders were not randomly assigned to program conditions (Lombard et al., 2004). Given the importance of the reentry problem and the success of handling other offender populations through the problem-solving court model, the costs and benefits of reentry courts is a subject that begs for more rigorous research.

It is critical to understand the impact of reentry courts on reoffending in comparison with traditional services. Without that information, one cannot determine how traditional parole agents can best interact with reentry court judges, whether the public will accept and community-based organizations will give priority to services for parolees when other needy populations need those same services, or whether state legislators will be willing to pay for the costs of reentry courts. As is the case for other specialized courts, it is necessary to determine whether it is the charismatic leadership of a judge and the interaction with the client that leads to desistance and other positive outcomes or a strict adherence to a sanctioning protocol. Another possibility is simply that clients are getting more substance abuse treatment and other services than they would have otherwise had. If the last situation is the case, then couldn't those enhanced services be provided by traditional parole agents rather than sitting court judges? These are all important questions in need of more rigorous research.

COMMUNITY CAPACITY

As a society, the United States has devoted relatively little thought and resources to helping people make the transition from the very structured system that characterizes prisons to freedom of movement and independent decision making in communities. And although the capacity of communities to which releasees return vary, most of them are inadequately prepared to assist formerly incarcerated people in making prosocial decisions, acquiring needed skills, and having the kind of opportunities (e.g., substance abuse treatment, employment counseling, and family reunification) that support successful reentry. A high proportion of releasees go to communities that are actually negative environments, with high crime rates or extensive drug markets that represent real threats to successful reentry. In some instances, communities have been fundamentally weakened in three ways: by individuals' criminal activities, by their absence due to incarceration, and then by the burden of their return (Kubrin and Stewart 2005; Clear et al., 2005, Travis, 2005).

Community capacity for prisoner reentry refers to two types of capacity—social capacity and resource capacity. The role that communities can play in fostering successful reentry and desistance has been underestimated in most public policy discussions about former prisoners. Communities can facilitate behaviors that contribute to desistance when neighborhoods and broader communities try to reintegrate former prisoners into law-abiding roles. Success is more likely when releasees can readily find places to live, have supportive families, are offered employment or educational opportunities, and have a way to participate in noncriminal networks. Successful reentry is not something a former inmate achieves alone, but in the context of and with the support of personal and community institutions, such as families, churches, and employers.

Communities can also facilitate a return to criminal behavior by being unable or unwilling to provide support for releasees. Some communities can be characterized as disorganized, that is, social integration in them is low. The people in such communities are not closely connected by work, family, and institutions, so releasees are unlikely to receive the kind of support that facilitates successful reentry. Rather, such neighborhoods are likely to have crime-conducive activity and networks that a former prisoner can too easily return to—the same or similar activity and behavior that led to the person's incarceration.

The importance of an "integrated," strong community as a regulator of behavior is an old idea in the social sciences (Bursik and Grasmick 1993; Shaw and McKay, 1969). In the last decade or so, renewed consideration of this idea has focused on collective efficacy—the capacity of a group of people in a neighborhood to work together to solve problems or otherwise take actions that affect their collective circumstances (Sampson et al., 1997). That is, a community uses its collective "social capital"—the links and networks between residents—for collective good.

An important facet of collective good is social control, of both residents and visitors or newcomers to the community. Neighborhood collective efficacy reduces neighborhood crime (Sampson, Raudenbush, and Earls, 1997). Residents in these communities actively participate in the informal social control that is a vital part of crime control. In some instances, such efforts support the efforts of police. Residents may take note of strangers and problematic behavior and situations, such as abandoned cars or drug dealing, and they take action. The police, in turn, respond to and support such efforts. The behavior and actions of releasees who return to such a community should be positively affected by these kinds of informal social control, as well as formal social controls. When collective efficacy is weak, new releasees, like other people in the community, are less regulated by informal social controls, and their chances for reinvolvement in criminal behavior are likely to be higher. The impact of collective efficacy on the criminal behavior of returning prisoners, as distinct from crime generally, is an important topic for future research.

Many releasees return to the same or similar communities as those they lived in prior to incarceration (e.g., Visher and Farrell, 2005). They choose to live there because those are the places where their families and friends live and where they can find housing. In many cases, those communities are disorganized ones. Even when releasees choose to live in new neighborhoods to avoid the people or situations that led to their incarceration, the new neighborhoods are generally similar to the old ones, disorganized and with low collective efficacy (Visher et al., 2004).

Moreover, when large numbers of former prisoners live close together in a community, they contribute to low collective efficacy because they are less likely to be employed, have lower incomes, and have fewer networks of people and institutions to support law-abiding behaviors (Clear et al., 2005). Ironically, the communities that may be the most accepting of releasees may also be the places that are the least likely to exercise social control. They are often communities with high rates of crime and substance use, which limit the possibilities for releasees' successful reentry. Releasees who report living in neighborhoods in "unsafe" or disorganized communities or where drug dealing is common are more likely to report using drugs after release, are less likely to be employed, and are more likely to return to prison than other releasees (Visher and Farrell, 2005).

Most people—including parole agents and corrections officials—believe that releasees who are employed have a higher probability of successful reentry, and research shows that employment does reduce recidivism (Bushway and Reuter, 2002). Yet people with prison records are much less likely to be offered jobs (Pager, 2003; Pager and Quillian, 2005) and are more likely to live in neighborhoods where others are out of work (Clear, 2007). At the same time, communities with more unemployed or marginally employed people have lower collective efficacy than other communities (Crutchfield et al., 2006; Fagan et al., 2006) and higher crime rates (Crutchfield, 1989). There is also some evidence from research on restorative justice and the involvement of victims in mediation conferences and other participatory activities that the involvement of citizens in the criminal justice process has positive effects on participants and may be therapeutic for releasees. Given opportunities to interact positively with others in activities that benefit the community, former prisoners begin to see themselves as part of something, a community (Maruna, 2001).

Often overlooked in reentry policies and practices are the institutions—including police, business sector, and health and human services—that can play important roles in successful reentry. The business community is not often involved in local discussions about the problems of crime and reentry, yet business is the source of money and jobs that could contribute to supporting communitywide reentry programs. Through a communitywide strategic planning process, Baltimore and Chicago have brought the business community into these discussions, and business leaders have responded by offering jobs to former prisoners (see, e.g., http://www.oedworks.com/whatsnew/pr0912202.htm [accessed June 2007]).

Of particular concern is how these institutions coordinate hiring policies, on-the-job or other employment training, eligibility for services, and decision making about parole revocation. Often these institutions are unaware of one another's policies and practices, which create inefficiencies and obstacles for former prisoners. In addition, some of these institutions may not have the institutional capacity to provide services to releasees, or they may not be familiar with the special problems of this population. This gap in the capacity of service providers is difficult to address, but it is a complaint often voiced by community residents when asked what should be done to support former prisoners in their transition from prison to local community (Visher and Farrell, 2005).

6

Conclusions, Recommendation, and Research Agenda

Two major conclusions emerge from our review of research on parole and desistance from crime. The first is that desistance from crime varies widely among parolees. Released prisoners with lengthy criminal records and who have been to prison several times before have very high recidivism rates—over 80 percent are rearrested within three years of release from prison. In contrast, less than half of first-time releasees and older releasees are rearrested within three years of their release (Langan and Levin, 2002; Rosenfeld et al., 2005; Solomon, Kachnowski, and Bhati, 2005). Indeed, when it comes to desistance or recidivism, there is no such thing as the "average" parolee. In a word, the parolee population is heterogeneous. It follows that the types of services, sanctions, and supervision strategies effective in increasing desistance among some groups of parolees may not be effective for other groups.

The second conclusion that emerges from our review of research on recidivism and desistance concerns intervention effects. We define "intervention" broadly to include both the routine functions of the criminal justice system (e.g., parole supervision) and the characteristics of discrete programs and treatments (e.g., drug abuse treatment). With some exceptions, the characteristics of interventions, including parole supervision itself, that are effective in increasing parolees' desistance from crime are unknown. This is not the same as saying that "nothing works" in reducing recidivism or increasing desistance (Farabee, 2005; Martinson, 1974); existing research knowledge is too thin to support that strong conclusion. In Petersilia's (2004) review of the prisoner reentry programs, she estimates that less than

1 percent of all prisoner reentry programs implemented in the United States in the last decade have been subject to a formal evaluation, and the vast majority of those did not use a randomized experimental research design. She writes that "using this 'body' of research to conclude anything about which reentry programs 'work' or 'don't work' seems misguided" (2004, p. 7). A major impediment to knowledge about "what works" in increasing desistance is poor program implementation. Without proper implementation, as well as careful evaluation, one cannot determine whether a given program succeeds or fails in its conception, design, or operation.

These two themes of parolee heterogeneity and intervention effects frame our summary of what is known and what needs to be learned about the characteristics of parolees and of the programs and interventions intended to increase their desistance from crime. In addition to our summary of the research findings on parolees and desistance programs and our proposed agenda for future research on parolees and their desistance from crime, we offer a policy recommendation that is driven by the research findings.

WHAT IS KNOWN ABOUT PAROLEES AND DESISTANCE

We use a comparatively permissive criterion for classifying a given research finding on parolees and programs as established or settled "knowledge." We include a research result in the category of "known" if it has been replicated across several studies and is not (or not any longer) subject to widespread dispute in the research community. A more restrictive criterion, for example, that any of the studies producing the result must meet the rigorous requirements of experimental science, would yield a much leaner knowledge base on the characteristics of parolees and effective programs. The difference is analogous to that between the "preponderance of evidence" and "beyond a reasonable doubt" evidentiary standard in jurisprudence. We adopt the former for organizing the extant research on parolees and desistance; however, for future research, we propose that, when feasible, it should be conducted and interpreted according to more rigorous standards of proof.

The need for more rigorous research methods in evaluating both prerelease and postrelease programs is beyond dispute, but the use of random designs does raise ethical questions in an environment that combines intervention and social control objectives. For example, a positive drug test typically triggers a sanction in most jurisdictions. Are treatments more restrictive or likelier to result in official sanctions than baseline parole conditions? These kinds of issues need to be thought out carefully in the design of experimental research. However, research suggests that ethical randomized designs are possible, especially where there is a standard program that can serve as a control for other randomized treatment groups, that is, in a situation where no one would get less than the standard postrelease treatment (see, for example, National Research Council, 2001).

Heterogeneity in the Parole Population

Recidivism rates, defined as the probability that parolees are rearrested or returned to prison, are significantly different for different groups of parolees. They are lower for women than for men; lower for older than younger parolees; lower for people with relatively short criminal records; and lower for violent offenders than for property or drug offenders (Langan and Levin, 2002; Petersilia, 2003).

Black parolees have higher recidivism rates than white parolees for violent and property crime, but not for drug crimes (Rosenfeld et al., 2005; see, also, Langan and Levin, 2002; Solomon et al., 2005). We note, however, that the race difference in recidivism is smaller than the race difference in overall arrest or imprisonment rates.

Parolees released from prison for the first time have lower recidivism rates than those who have been released in the past and then returned to prison. This finding holds even when sex, age, race, criminal record, offense type, and other characteristics of parolees are controlled (Rosenfeld et al., 2005; Tonry, 2004). The cause of this difference has not been established, however. Selection may play a major role; past failure at reentry predicts future failure. It also is possible that parole authorities and the police supervise and watch "two-time losers" more closely or are less willing to overlook any violations of their parole contracts. The finding that past imprisonment predicts future rearrest and imprisonment is consistent with the idea that the prison experience itself is criminogenic, but, recidivism does not appear to be related to the length of time an individual spends in prison (Rosenfeld et al., 2005). Another possibility is that people who have been imprisoned multiple times possess unmeasured traits or deficits that impede desistance. At present, the simple conclusion one can draw from what is known is that past recidivism predicts future recidivism.

One of the most significant findings that emerges from our work is that the peak rates for recidivism occur in the days and weeks immediately following release. Arrest rates decline over time after release from prison, especially for property and drug crimes. Moreover, death rates for new releasees—within the first days and weeks—are much higher than for matched demographic groups in the general population. This is a new research finding, the importance of which is underscored by the fact that the causes of death for parolees and inmates are different. For the state prison population, the leading causes of death are disease related: cardiovascular disease, cancer, liver diseases, and AIDS-related illnesses. For the releasee population in the state of Washington, by contrast, the four leading causes of death were drug overdose, cardiovascular disease, homicide, and suicide. Two of these, homicide and drug overdose, are directly related to risky behaviors, and all may be preventable if close attention and intensive services are given to these releasees at the time of release.

Parolees are characterized by a range of deficits in a number of areas. Large fractions of them have educational and cognitive deficits, substance abuse and mental health problems, inadequate housing, and difficulties in finding and keeping a job (Petersilia, 2003; Travis, 2005). A clear need exists for appropriate support services and treatment for people reentering the community from prison with these deficits. Adequate research on specific elements such as the nature, timing, and dosage of services has not been conducted. Research on this population and on the effects of such interventions is the only way to establish whether the absence or inadequacy of services for released prisoners is causally related to recidivism.

Formal and Informal Controls

The limited research that has been done shows that formal parole supervision has only a small effect on recidivism. However, we again must caution against drawing a broad conclusion on the basis of existing research, which is methodologically weak and masks large differences in local variations in supervision and services received by parolees. The effect of parole on recidivism appears to be a function of selection of prisoners for release rather than supervision in the community. Controlling for sex, race, age, criminal history, and other factors, parolees released through a discretionary process have a lower recidivism rate than those subject to mandatory release—even though both groups experience generally the same conditions of supervision in the community (Rosenfeld et al., 2005). The effects of parole supervision, however, differ for different groups of parolees. Parole supervision appears to reduce the recidivism rates of parolees who are comparatively low risk (e.g., women and parolees with shorter criminal records), but has little effect on the recidivism rate of higher risk parolees (Solomon, 2005, 2006).

Informal social controls, such as marriage and work, are more effective than formal social controls, such as parole supervision and rearrest, in increasing desistance from crime in ways that are generally similar across crime types. Comparatively strong evidence exists regarding the causal effect on criminal behavior of informal social control, especially marriage. Married men are less likely than unmarried men to commit crimes, and recent research has extended this finding to women (King et al., 2007; Griffin and Armstrong, 2003) The effect of marriage on criminal behavior persists even when the traits that predispose men to marry are controlled

(Laub and Sampson, 2003; Sampson et al., 2006; King et al., 2007). The marriage findings for females are more ambiguous. Whether the marriage effect on criminal behavior applies specifically to parolees is not known.

Intervention Effects

Several kinds of intervention programs have been carried out and studied enough for some conclusions to be drawn, although, as noted above, the quality of implementation in these programs is often wanting. The research does show that the effectiveness of interventions to increase desistance from crime depends heavily on implementation characteristics, including staff quality and training, program length and intensity, and organizational readiness. Moreover, few successful interventions have been "manualized."

The effects of in-prison programs on recidivism are rather small. In-prison programs have larger effects on recidivism when coupled with postrelease community-based programs. Among psychological therapeutic approaches for reducing criminal behavior, cognitive-behavioral therapeutic approaches are more effective than other approaches in reducing recidivism. For substance abuse, treatment appears to reduce criminal behavior, at least during the period a person is in treatment. However, it is not clear whether this result applies to parolees specifically. It is clear that treatment for substance abuse is more effective in reducing recidivism in combination with criminal justice supervision than either treatment or supervision alone. Criminal offenders under legal pressure to undergo substance abuse treatment have higher attendance rates and remain in treatment longer than those entering treatment voluntarily (National Institute on Drug Abuse, 2006).

RESEARCH AGENDA

The research literature raises more questions than it answers about the characteristics of parolees and the effects of interventions on desistance. For that reason, our list of questions to guide future research is longer than our list of research findings. The topics are not in order of priority.

As with our description of what is known, we divide the proposed research agenda into questions about the heterogeneity of parolees and those on the effects of interventions in reducing recidivism and increasing desistance from crime. We have not aimed for exhaustiveness in framing the agenda, but rather have emphasized those questions that arise most directly from the existing research. Nonetheless, answers to these questions would greatly enhance knowledge about desistance from crime and the characteristics of interventions that increase desistance. In addition, continuing research is needed on how to develop and standardize measures of desistance, a more complex concept than recidivism. The committee believes that research on community supervision and desistance from crime should constitute a major research priority of the National Institute of Justice and of private organizations that fund criminal justice research.

Understanding Parole Heterogeneity

Early Failure

Early failure is a high research priority if recidivism is to be reduced and desistance supported and encouraged. Does the fact that much recidivism occurs in the first days after release mean that people predisposed to fail usually fail quickly or that those days are especially risky for all released prisoners? How do parolees who fail early differ from those who fail later? Is motivation to succeed a key factor and if so, what kinds of programs and policies could support such motivation? More data are needed on the individual characteristics of persons who fail on parole.

Recidivism Rates

Recidivism rates can be seen as one measure of the failure to desist from crime. What drives this failure? Are the higher recidivism rates of parolees with multiple imprisonments a function of selection (a predisposition to fail among those who have failed before), the consequence of the criminogenic effects of imprisonment, the consequences of community characteristics, or the result of undetected individual traits?

Special Populations

What kinds of services will best meet the needs of specific groups of parolees in the future, such as women or elderly releasees? Why are racial and ethnic disparities in the rearrest and reincarceration of parolees different from (lower than) disparities in initial police contacts, arrests, convictions, and prison sentences?

Informal Social Controls

How do the effects of informal social control differ over the course of criminal careers? Do the known effects of marriage on desistance specifically hold for parolees? What forms of informal control are most effective with younger parolees with high expected recidivism rates and low marriage rates? What drives the low rates of formal marriage among this population and what could be done to increase rates of formal marriage? What dynamics underlie the difference in outcomes of marriage and cohabitation in relation to crime? How can parole take advantage of and leverage "naturally occurring" guardians in the community, such as spouses, parents, neighbors, and employers?

Community Effects on Parolees

What are the effects of neighborhood or community conditions—such as the presence of high crime rates or drug markets or the availability, or lack thereof, of social and treatment services—on parolees? Should prison and parole authorities consider relocating released prisoners away from communities with high levels of crime or other characteristics that impede desistance? Should such relocation strategies be considered only for released prisoners who do not have strong family or other social ties to their "home" communities? What would be the effects of relocation?

Parolee Effects on Communities

What are the effects of parolees on the crime rates of the communities (neighborhoods and cities) to which they return after release from prison? There are just two studies on the effects of released prisoners on state arrest rates (Rosenfeld et al., 2005; Raphael and Stoll, 2004). Do the findings also apply to local communities? Does the impact of parolees on local crime rates (if any) differ by crime type (i.e., violent crime, property crime, drug crime)?

Intervention Effects

Interventions can only be effective if they are affordable and can be implemented competently. Moreover, most postrelease interventions are viewed as adding costs to an already expensive system: thus, the cost of implementing reentry programs that build on research or even of conducting the research itself creates a formidable obstacle to the kinds of changes we propose. Yet a number of studies have shown that these costs are far lower than the incarceration costs that are currently being incurred by parolees who have been returned to prison and are expected in the future (Aos et al., 2001; Castellano and Riker, 2001). A new report from the Pew Foundation (2007) forecasts that state and federal prison populations will grow by more than 192,000 inmates: these prisoners alone could cost as much as $27.5 billion in new operating and construction costs.

The new costs will not be evenly distributed across states. For example, 18 percent of all parolees in the United States are in California (Zhang et al., 2006). Moreover, a higher proportion of inmates in the future are likely to be female or elderly; both groups have special needs and higher costs. Enhanced penalties for certain kinds of offenders promise to raise costs as well. The committee believes that developing strong reentry programs that lower reoffending, rearrest, and reincarceration rates is critical to lowering these costs. Research on interventions should include cost effectiveness studies and should suggest how cost savings in terms of reduced prison costs could be realized.

Effects of Prerelease Planning

What kinds of reentry issues and problems are considered when developing the prerelease plan? How can needs be prioritized to prevent early failure or death? How well are prerelease plans followed by the parole officer and releasee over the course of the parole period? How do prerelease plans interact with availability and accessibility of services?

Effects of Parole

Prior efforts to improve parole programs have neglected one of the core functions—the role of the parole or probation supervision officer. Solomon and her colleagues (2005) have shown that formal parole supervision has limited effects: Why, then, are the recidivism effects of parole greater for some groups than for others? What is the role of agency culture and parole officers' orientation and training? What is the contribution of a community's capacity (e.g., program availability, resources) to foster desistance? What kinds of parole officer training are required when implementing new approaches or managing individualized re-entry plans for releasees?

Designing Interventions

Given the heterogeneity of the parolee population, what can be done to ensure that parolees are appropriately matched with specific interventions? Are there general programs (e.g., education and literacy programs, family-focused supervision) that are effective with all parolees? How effective in reducing recidivism and increasing desistance from crime are "triage" approaches that concentrate services and treatments on lower risk parolees and intensify supervision for higher risk released prisoners? How effective are strength-based approaches in increasing desistance from crime?

Timing Interventions

Recent research on how the timing of surveillance, supervision, and services affect recidivism and desistance needs to be replicated and extended. Which interventions are most effective when introduced immediately after release from prison? Would it be better to begin certain reentry services and treatments prior to release from prison? If so, at what point during imprisonment should such interventions begin (e.g., a year before release, 6 months, 3 months)? How should they be connected to interventions in the community?

Comprehensive Approaches

Do comprehensive, multilevel strategies (involving community or organizational change) produce significant reductions in recidivism? What types of community or organizational change are most effective?

Effects of Restrictions on Releasees

How do policies that restrict the access of released prisoners to public housing and other forms of public assistance—including treatment services, educational benefits, and other resources—affect desistance from crime?

Role of Technology

How effective are technological innovations, such as computerized reporting, electronic monitoring, and global positioning system (GPS) monitoring, in improving compliance with parole requirements and desistance from crime? For which offenders (e.g., sex offenders, gang members) is the technology warranted? Are such innovations cost-effective when compared with the traditional practices they supplement or replace?

Sanctions for Parole Violation

Do stringent special conditions in parole contracts cause parolees to fail? Are low-level sanctions, such as short stays in jail, for violating the conditions of parole effective in reducing the commission of new crimes? Should such sanctions be graduated in severity for subsequent violations, or are constant sanctions as effective as graduated sanctions in maintaining compliance with parole requirements and desistance from crime? What are the costs and benefits of alternative policies for technical violation on the overall justice system, crime, and criminal desistance?

Incentives for Parolees

How can incentives be used along with negative sanctions to ensure that released prisoners comply with parole requirements and to encourage desistance from crime? What types of incentives (e.g., shortening the length of parole, relaxation of certain requirements) are most effective? What is the benefit of state issued "certificates of rehabilitation" in fostering desistance?

System Incentives

What types of incentives are most effective in improving the morale and performance of parole officers and system response to released prisoners? Would a regime that ties organizational rewards to improved monitoring, service delivery, and compliance with parole requirements spur organizational innovation? Can such a system increase desistance from crime by parolees in comparison with traditional parole procedures and practices?

Measurement and Methods

Measurement Issues

How valid are arrests, technical violations, and other recidivism indicators as measures of desistance from crime among parolees? How well do violations of the technical requirements of community supervision predict the commission of new crimes? To what degree do recidivism measures, such as arrests, confound criminal offending with the system response to offending? Are conventional recidivism indicators more valid for some groups of parolees than others?

Methods

As this review unmistakably demonstrates, the application of scientifically rigorous methods in research and evaluation on community supervision has not been the norm and is only now beginning to emerge. Inadequate implementation of program principles and procedures appears to be a significant obstacle in the way of program effectiveness or of finding out whether a program might have benefits for participants. A major limitation of current program evaluation results is the failure to account fully for self-selection bias. Random assignment of persons to treatment and control conditions remains rare in research on the reentry process. What kinds of experimental evaluation and cost effectiveness studies could be designed and implemented to address and improve this situation? What methods are most appropriate and how can barriers to using them (i.e. implementation, security, or ethics issues) be addressed and overcome?

RECOMMENDATION

The new work that confirms long-standing research findings on the high rates of recidivism and the risk of death in the first weeks and months after release from prison lead the committee to make a recommendation regarding policies and programs for parolees and other releasees.

The committee recommends that parole authorities and administrators of both in-prison and postrelease programs redesign their activities and programs to provide major support to parolees and other releasees at the time of release. These interventions should be subjected to rigorous evaluation.

Given the paucity of rigorous evidence about the effectiveness of many intervention programs or the motivation underlying individual change, the committee can offer only limited advice about what specific form some of these programs should take. **Cognitive-behavioral approaches have strong scientific support and the committee believes that they should be widely implemented and continually evaluated, especially taking account of program implementation issues.** Drug treatment coupled with frequent testing for drug use also shows evidence of lowering recidivism. Several other programs and approaches show promise in reducing violations of community supervision requirements, arrests for new crimes, and drug use. Included here are programs that focus on individual change and motivation, and comprehensive, multiservice employment and training initiatives.

"Nothing works" is no longer a defensible conclusion from assessments of program effects on reentry outcomes. When a person leaves prison it is clear that he or she has needs an immediate place to live, a person such as a case manager to facilitate the immediate transition from prison to the community, and a program to guide postrelease life. However, we cannot identify with confidence other best practices for reducing recidivism and enhancing desistance among people returning to local communities from prison. Because so few reentry service programs are accompanied by rigorous evaluations, a scientific review panel, such as this committee, has very little to draw on with confidence (see National Research Council, 1979, for a history of this problem). Yet there is a great deal of experiential and practitioner knowledge with regard to the apparent efficacy of various programs (Wilkinson, 2004). The challenge over the next decade, as prisoner reentry, parole, and desistance from crime become even more important, is to subject these promising practices to rigorously designed evaluations.

References

Adams, K., K.J. Bennett, T.J. Flanagan, J.W. Marquart, S.J. Cuvelier, E. Fritsch, J. Gerber, D.R. Longmire, and V.S. Burton, Jr. (1994). A large-scale multidimensional test of the effect of prison education programs on offenders' behavior. *Prison Journal, 74,* 443-449.

Adams, D., and J. Fischer. (1976).The effects of prison residents' community contacts on recidivism rates. *Corrective and Social Psychiatry, 22,* 21-27.

Andrews, D.A., and J. Bonta. (1994). *The psychology of criminal conduct.* Cincinnati, OH: Anderson.

Andrews, D., and J. Bonta. (1998). *Psychology of criminal conduct, second edition.* Cincinnati, OH: Anderson.

Andrews, D.A., and J. Bonta. (2003). *The psychology of criminal conduct, third edition.* Cincinnati, OH: Anderson.

Andrews, D.A., I. Zinger, R.D. Hoge, J. Bonta, P. Gendreau, and F.T. Cullen. (1990). Does correctional treatment work?: A clinically relevant and psychologically informed meta analysis. *Criminology, 28*(3), 369-404.

Aos, S., M. Miller, and E. Drake. (2006). *Evidence-based adult corrections programs: What works and what does not.* Olympia: Washington State Institute for Public Policy.

Aos, S., P. Phipps, R. Barnoski, and A. Lieb. (2001). *The comparative costs and benefits of programs to reduce crime.* Olympia: Washington State Institute for Public Policy.

Bhati, A. (2007). *Studying the effects of incarceration on offending trajectories: A theoretic approach.* Available at http://www.urban.org/url.cfm?ID=411427 (accessed March 28, 2007).

Bandura, A. (1977). *Social learning theory.* Englewood Cliffs, NJ: Prentice-Hall.

Barton, W.H. (2006). Incorporating the strengths perspective into juvenile aftercare. *Western Criminology Review, 7*(2), 48-61.

Beck, J.S. (1995). *Cognitive therapy: Basics and beyond.* New York: Guilford.

Berk, R.A., K.J. Lenihan, and P.H. Rossi. (1980). Crime and poverty: Some experimental evidence from ex-offenders. *American Sociology Review, 45,* 766-786.

Binswanger, I.A., M.F. Stern, R.A. Deyo, P.J. Heagerty, A. Cheadle, J.G. Elmore, and T.C. Koepsell. (2007). Release from prison—A high risk of death for former inmates. *New England Journal of Medicine, 356*(2), 157-165. [See also erratum, *New England Journal of Medicine, 356*(5), 536.]

Blumstein, A., and A. Beck. (2005). Reentry as a transient state between liberty and commitment. In J. Allen, J. Travis, and C. Visher (Eds.), *Prisoner reentry and crime in America* (pp. 50-79). New York: Cambridge University Press.

Boudin, K. (1993). Participatory literacy education behind bars. *Harvard Educational Review, 63*(2), 207-232.

Brame, R., S.D. Bushway, and R. Paternoster. (2003). Examining the prevalence of criminal desistance. *Criminology, 41,* 423-448.

Branch, A., and J. Tierney. (2000). *Big Brother Big Sister impact study.* Philadelphia: Public/Private Ventures.

Brewer, A. (2001). *Impact of hepatitis C on deaths in Massachusetts DOC from 1995-2000.* Paper presented at the 25th National Conference on Correctional Health Care, November 12, Albuquerque, NM. Available from the author, Correctional Medical Services, Inc., St. Louis, MO 63141.

Broome, K.M., K. Knight, M.L. Hiller, and D.D. Simpson. (1996). Drug treatment process indicators for probationers and prediction of recidivism. *Journal of Substance Abuse Treatment, 13*(6), 487-491.

Brownell, K.D., G.A. Marlatt, E. Lichtenstein, and G.T. Wilson. (1986). Understanding and preventing relapse. *American Psychologist, 41,* 765-782.

Buck, M.L. (2000). *Getting back to work: Employment programs for ex-offenders.* Field Report Series. Philadelphia: Public/Private Ventures.

Bureau of Justice Statistics. (1994). *Drugs and crime facts.* Available at http://www.ojp.usdoj.gov/bjs/dcf/contents.htm (accessed May 25, 2007).

Bureau of Justice Statistics. (2002). *National Corrections Reporting Program: Time served in state prison by offense, release type, gender, and race.* Available at http://www.ojp.usdoj.gov/bjs/dtdata.htm (accessed July 25, 2007).

Bureau of Justice Statistics. (2006a) *Probation and parole statistics: Summary findings.* Available at http://www.ojp.usdoj.gov/bjs/pandp.htm (accessed September 2006).

Bureau of Justice Statistics. (2006b). *Reentry trends in the United States: Inmates returning to the community after serving time in prison.* Available at http://www.ojp.usdoj.gov/bjs/reentry/reentry.htm (accessed September 2006).

Burnett, R., and S. Maruna. (2004). *Prisoners as citizens' advisors: The OxCab-Springhill Partnership and its wider implications.* (Final evaluation report). London, England: Esmee Fairbairn Foundation.

Burrell, W. (2005). Trends in probation and parole in the states. In Council of State Governments, *Book of the states, 2005.* Lexington, KY: Council of State Governments.

Bursik, R.J., Jr., and H. Grasmick. (1993). *Neighborhoods and crime: The dimensions of effective community control.* New York: Lexington.

Bushway, S.D., and P. Reuter. (2002). Labor markets and crime. In J.Q. Wilson and J. Petersilia (Eds.), *Crime: Public policies for crime control.* Oakland, CA: ICS Press.

Bushway, S.D., T.P. Thornberry, and M.D. Krohn. (2003). Desistance as a developmental process: A comparison of static and dynamic approaches. *Journal of Quantitative Criminology, 19,* 129-153.

Bushway, S.D., A.R. Piquero, L.M. Briody, E. Cauffman, and P. Mazerolle. (2001). An empirical framework for studying desistance as a process. *Criminology, 39,* 491-513.

California Legislative Analyst's Office. (2004). *Analysis of the 2004-2005 budget bill.* Available at http://www.lao.ca.gov/analysis_2004/crim_justice/cj_07_5240_anl04.htm#_Toc64089220 (accessed June 22, 2007).

Cartier, J., D. Farabee, and M. Pendergast. (2006). Methamphetamine use, self-reported violent crime, and recidivism among offenders in California who abuse substances. *Journal of Interpersonal Violence, 21*(4), 435-445.

Casey, P.A., and D.B. Rottman. (2003). *Problem-solving courts: Models and trends.* Williamsburg, VA: National Center for State Courts. Available at http://www.ncsconline.org/WC/Publications/COMM_ProSolProbSolvCtsPub.pdf (accessed November 2006).

Castellano, U.A., and A. Riker. (2000). *Community-based treatment: Impact of the Homeless Pretrial Release Project.* San Francisco, CA: Center on Juvenile and Criminal Justice. Available at http://www.cjcj.org/pubs/hrp/hrp.html (accessed July 2007).

Center for Substance Abuse Prevention. (2000). *Mentoring initiatives: An overview of mentoring.* Washington, DC: U.S. Department of Health and Human Services.

Clark, J.R., and D.R. Lee. (2005). Leadership, prisonersí dilemmas, and politics. *Cato Journal, 25*(2), 379-397.

Clear, T.R. (2007) *Imprisoning communities: How mass incarceration makes disadvantaged neighborhoods worse.* New York: Oxford University Press.

Clear, T.R., E. Waring, and K. Scully. (2005). Communities and reentry: Concentrated reentry cycling. In J. Travis and C. Visher (Eds.), *Prisoner reentry and crime in America.* New York: Cambridge University Press.

Cohen, L.E., and M. Felson. (1979). Social change and crime rate trends: A routine activity approach. *American Sociological Review, 44,* 588-608.

Cohen, M.A., T.R. Rust, S. Steen, and S. Tidd. (2004). Willingness to pay for crime control programs. *Criminology, 42*(1), 86-106.

Compton, W., L. Cottler, J. Jacobs, A. Ben-Abdallah, and E. Spitznagel. (2003). The role of psychiatric disorders in predicting drug dependence treatment outcomes. American *Journal of Psychiatry, 160,* 890-895.

Cook, P., and J. Ludwig. (2000). *Gun violence: The real costs.* New York: Oxford University Press.

Cready, C.M., M.A. Fossett, and K.J. Kiecolt. (1997). Mate availability and African American family structure in the U.S. nonmetropolitan south, 1960-1990. *Journal of Marriage and the Family, 59,* 192-203.

Cressy, D.R. (1955). Changing criminals: The application of the theory of differential association. *The American Journal of Sociology, 61*(2), 116-120.

Crutchfield, R.D. (1989). Labor stratification and violent crime. *Social Forces, 68*(2), 489-512.

Crutchfield, R.D., R.L. Matsueda, and K. Drakulich. (2006). Race, labor markets, and neighborhood violence. In R. Peterson, L. Krivo, and J. Hagan (Eds.), *The color of crime.* New York: New York University Press.

Cullen, F.T., and P. Gendreau. (2000). Assessing correctional rehabilitation: Policy, practice, and prospects. In J. Horney (Ed.), *Criminal justice 2000* (vol. 3, pp. 109-176). Washington, DC: U.S. Department of Justice.

Davis, M.I., B.D. Olson, L.A. Jason, J. Alvarez, and J.R. Ferrari. (2006). Cultivating and maintaining effective action research partnerships: The DePaul and Oxford House collaborative. *Journal of Prevention and Intervention in the Community (Special Issue), 31*(1/2), 3-12.

DeJong, P., and I.K. Berg. (2002). *Interviewing for solutions, second edition.* Pacific Grove, CA: Brooks/Cole Thomson Learning.

Ditton, P. (1999). *Mental health and treatment of inmates and probationers.* Bureau of Justice Special Reports, Office of Justice Programs (NCJ #174463). Washington, DC: U.S. Department of Justice. Available at www.ojp.usdoj.gov/bjs/pub/mhtip/pdf (accessed October 2006).

Early, T.J., and L.F. GlenMaye. (2000). Valuing families: Social work practice with families from a strengths perspective. *Social Work, 45*, 118-133.

Ekland-Olson, S., M. Supanic, J. Campbell, and K.J. Lenihan. (1983). Postrelease depression and the importance of familial support. *Criminology, 21*(2), 253-275.

Ezell, M.E. (2007). Examining the overall and offense-specific criminal career lengths of a sample of serious offenders. *Crime and Delinquency, 53*, 3-37.

Ezell, M.E., and L.E. Cohen. (2005). *Desisting from crime: Continuity and change in long-term crime patterns of serious chronic offenders*. Oxford, England: Oxford University Press.

Fabelo, T. (2000). *Impact of educational achievement of inmates in the Windham School District on post-release employment*. Austin, TX: Criminal Justice Policy Council. Available at http://web.archive.org/web/20030507094851/http://www.cjpc.state.tx.us/reports/alphalist/wsdemploy10.pdf (accessed February 2007).

Fagan, J. (1989). Cessation of family violence: Deterrence and dissuasion. In L. Ohlin and M. Tonry (Eds.), *Family violence* (vol. 11, pp. 377-425). Chicago: University of Chicago Press.

Fagan J., A. Piquero, and V. West. (2006). Neighborhood, race, and the economic consequences of incarceration in New York City, 1985-1996. In R.D. Peterson and L.J. Krivo (Eds.), *The many colors of crime: Inequalities of race, ethnicity and crime in America*. New York: New York University Press.

Farabee, D. (2005). *Rethinking rehabilitation: Why can't we reform our criminals?* Washington, DC: AEI Press.

Farrall, S. (2002). Long-term absences from probation: Officers' and probationers' accounts. *Howard Journal of Criminal Justice, 41*(3), 263-278.

Farrall, S., and S. Maruna. (2004). Desistance-focused criminal justice policy research: Introduction to a special issue on desistance from crime and public policy. *Howard Journal, 43*(4), 358-367.

Farrington, D.P., and J.D. Hawkins. (1991). Predicting participation, early onset and later persistence in officially recorded offending. *Criminal Behavior and Mental Health, 1*, 1-33.

Farrington, D.P., and D.J. West. (1995). Effects of marriage, separation, and children on offending by adult males. In Z. Blau and J. Hagan (Eds.), *Current perspectives on aging and the life cycle* (vol. 4, pp. 249-281). Greenwich, CT: JAI Press.

Federal Bureau of Prisons. (2000). *Triad drug treatment evaluation project. Final report of three-year outcomes, Office of Research and Evaluation*. Washington, DC: Federal Bureau of Prisons, Office of Research and Evaluation. Available at http://www.bop.gov/news/research_reports.jsp#drug (accessed August 2007).

Finn, M.A., and S. Muirhead-Steves. (2002). The effectiveness of electronic monitoring with violent male parolees. *Justice Quarterly, 19*, 293-312.

Gendreau, P., and T. Little. (1993). *A meta-analysis of the effectiveness of sanctions on offender recidivism*. St. John, New Brunswick: University of New Brunswick.

Gaes, G.G., T.J. Flanagan, L.L. Motiuk, and L. Stewart. (1999). Adult correctional treatment. In M. Tonry and J. Petersilia (eds.), *Prisons*. Chicago: University of Chicago Press.

Gerber, J., and E.J. Fritsch. (1994). The effects of academic and vocational program participation on inmate misconduct and reincarceration. In *Prison education research project: Final report* (Ch. 3). Huntsville, TX: Sam Houston State University.

Giordano, P.C., S.A. Cernkovich, and J.L. Rudolph. (2002). Gender, crime, and desistance: Toward a theory of cognitive transformation. *American Journal of Sociology, 107*, 990-1064.

Glaser, D. (1969). *The effectiveness of a prison and parole system, abridged edition*. Indianapolis, IN: Bobbs-Merrill.

Glueck, S., and E. Glueck. (1974). *Of delinquency and crime.* Springfield, IL: Charles C. Thomas.

Gottfredson, M.R., and T. Hirschi. (1990). *A general theory of crime.* Stanford, CA: Stanford University Press.

Griffin, M., and G. Armstrong. (2003). The effect of local life circumstances on female probationersí offending. *Justice Quarterly, 20*(2), 213-239.

Grogger, J. (1998). Market wages and youth crime. *Journal of Labor Economics, 16*(4), 756-791.

Haapanen, R., L. Britton, and T. Croisdale. (2007). Persistent criminality and career length. *Crime and Delinquency, 53,* 133-155.

Hairston, C.F. (2002). The importance of families in prisoners' community reentry. *ICCA Journal on Community Corrections,* April, 11-14.

Hammett, T.M., C. Roberts, S. Kennedy, W. Rhodes, T. Conklin, T. Lincoln, and R.W. Tuthill. (2004). *Evaluation of the Hampden County public health model of correctional care.* (Final Report to the National Institute of Justice.) Cambridge, MA: Abt Associates.

Harer, M.D. (1995). *Prison education program participation and recidivism: A test of the normalization hypothesis.* (Federal Bureau of Prisons, Office of Research and Evaluation.) Washington, DC: U.S. Department of Justice.

Harrell, A., and J. Roman. (2001). Reducing drug use and crime among offenders: The impact of graduated sanctions. *Journal of Drug Issues, 31*(1), 207-232.

Harris, P.M., R. Gingerich, and T.A. Whittaker. (2004). The "effectiveness" of differential supervision. *Crime Delinquency, 50*(2), 235-271.

Harrison, P.M., and A.J. Beck. (2006). *Prisoners in 2005.* Washington, DC: U.S. Department of Justice.

Healy, K.M. (1999). *Case management in the criminal justice system.* National Institute of Justice (NCJ #173409). Washington, DC: U.S. Department of Justice.

Herrera, C., C.L. Sipe, and W.S. McClanahan. (2000). *Mentoring school-age children: Relationship development in community-based and school-based programs.* Philadelphia: Public/Private Ventures.

Herrera, C., Z. Vang, and L.Y. Gale. (2002). Group mentoring: A study of mentoring groups in three programs. Philadelphia: Public/Private Ventures.

Hiller, M.L., E. Narevic, C. Leukefeld, and J. Matthew. (2002). *Webster, Kentucky reentry courts: Evaluation of the pilot programs.* Williamsburg, VA: State Justice Institute.

Hindelang, M.J., M.R. Gottfredson, and J. Garofalo. (1978). *Victims of personal crime: An empirical foundation for a theory of personal victimization.* Cambridge, MA: Ballinger.

Holzer, H.J., and K. Martinson. (2005). *Can we improve job retention and advancement among low-income working parents?* Washington, DC: Urban Institute. Available at http://www.urban.org/url.cfm?ID=311241 (accessed September 2006).

Holzer, H., S. Raphael, and M. Stoll. (2001). *Will employers hire ex-offenders? Employer preferences, background checks, and their determinants.* (JCPR Working Paper #238). Chicago: Northwestern University/University of Chicago Joint Center for Poverty Research.

Horn, M. (2002). Keynote address to Corrections Technology Association, New Orleans (November). Available at http://www.correctionstech.org/2002Conference/Presentations/KeynoteAddress. pdf#search=%22Martin%20Horn%22 (accessed September 2006).

Horney, J., D.W. Osgood, and I.H. Marshall. (1995). Criminal careers in the short-term: Intra-individual variability in crime and its relation to local life circumstances. *American Sociological Review 60,* 655-673.

Hser, Y., M.E. Stark, A. Paredes, D. Huang, M.D. Anglin, and R. Rawson. (2006). A 12-year follow-up of a treated cocaine dependent sample. *Journal of Substance Abuse Treatment, 30*(3), 219-226.

Hughes, T.A., D.J. Wilson, and A.J. Beck. (2001). *Trends in state parole, 1990-2000*. Washington, DC: U.S. Department of Justice, Bureau of Justice Statistics.

Irwin, J. (1970). *The felon*. Englewood Cliffs, NJ: Prentice Hall.

Jacobson, M. (2005). *Downsizing prisons: How to reduce crime and end mass incarceration*. New York: New York University Press.

James, D.J., and L.E. Glaze. (2006). *Mental health problems of prison and jail inmates*. Washington, DC: U.S. Department of Justice.

Jason, L.A., B.D. Olson, J.R. Ferrari, and T. LoSasso. (2006). A randomized, longitudinal evaluation of communal housing settings for substance abuse recovery. *American Journal of Public Health, 96*(10), 1727-1729.

Jenkins, W., Jr., R.R. Griswold, and B.E. Gillespie. (1993). *Prison inmates: better plans needed before felons are released*. Washington, DC: U.S. General Accounting Office.

Johnson, B.R. (1984). *Hellfire and corrections: A quantitative study of Florida prison inmates*. Ph.D. dissertation, School of Criminology, Florida State University.

Jolliffe, D., and D. Farrington. (2007). *A rapid evidence assessment of the impact of mentoring on offending: A summary*. Home Office Online Report available at http://www.homeoffice.gov.uk/rds/pdfs07/rdsolr1107.pdf (accessed May 31, 2007).

Jucovy, L. (2006). *Just out: Early lessons from the Ready4Work Prisoner Reentry Initiative*. Philadelphia: Public/Private Ventures.

Kaminer, Y. (2004). Contingency management reinforcement procedures for adolescent substance abuse. *Journal of the American Academy of Child and Adolescent Psychiatry, 39*, 1324-1326.

Karburg, J.C., and D.J. James. (2005) *Substance dependence, abuse, and treatment of jail inmates, 2002*. (Bureau of Justice Statistics Special Report, Office of Justice Programs.) Washington, DC: U.S. Department of Justice. Available at http://www.ojp.usdoj.gov/bjs/sdatji02.pdf (accessed October 2006).

Kazemian, L. (2007). Desistance from crime: Theoretical, empirical, methodological, and policy considerations. *Journal of Contemporary Criminal Justice, 23*, 1, [Special Issue on Desistance, Lila Kazemian and David Farrington, Eds.]

King, R.D., M. Massoglia, and R. MacMillan. (2007). The context of marriage and crime: Gender, the propensity to marry, and offending in early adulthood. *Criminology, 45*, 33-64.

Kinnon, J.B. (2003) The shocking state of black marriage: Experts say many will never get married. *Ebony*, November.

Kruttschnitt, C., C. Uggen, and K. Shelton. (2000). Predictors of desistance among sex offenders: The intersection of formal and informal social controls. *Justice Quarterly, 17*, 61-87.

Kubrin, C., and E. Stewart. (2005). Predicting who reoffends: the neglected role of neighborhood context in recidivism studies. *Criminology, 44*(1), 165-197.

Landenberger, N.A., and M. Lipsey. (2006). The positive effects of cognitive-behavioral programs for offenders: A meta-analysis of factors associated with effective treatment. *Journal of Experimental Criminology, 1*(4), 435-450.

Langan, P.A., and D.J. Levin. (2002). *Recidivism of prisoners released in 1994*. Washington, DC: U.S. Department of Justice.

Lattimore, P.K. (2006). *Triage: Resource allocation for probation and parole*. Paper prepared for Committee on Community Supervision and Desistance from Crime Workshop, Jan., National Research Council, Washington, DC.

Laub, J.H., and L.C. Allen. (1999). Life course criminology and community corrections. *Texas Probation, 14*, 11-21.

Laub, J.H., and R.J. Sampson. (1993). Turning points in the life course: Why change matters to the study of crime. *Criminology, 31*, 301-325.

Laub, J.H., and R.J. Sampson. (2001). Understanding desistance from crime. In M. Tonry (Ed.), *Crime and justice: A review of research* (vol. 28, pp. 1-69). Chicago: University of Chicago Press.

Laub, J.H., and R.J. Sampson. (2003). *Shared beginnings, divergent lives: Delinquent boys to age 70.* Cambridge, MA: Harvard University Press.

Laub, J.H., D.S. Nagin, and R.J. Sampson. (1998). Trajectories of change in criminal offending: Good marriages and the desistance process. *American Sociological Review, 63*, 225-238.

La Vigne, N., and J. Cowan. (2005). *Mapping prisoner reentry: An action research guidebook.* Washington, DC: The Urban Institute Justice Policy Center.

La Vigne, N.G., C. Visher, and J. Castro. (2004). *Chicago prisoners' reflections on returning home.* Washington, DC: Urban Institute.

La Vigne, N.G., A.L. Solomon, K.A. Beckman, and K. Dedel. (2006). *Prisoner reentry and community policing: Strategies for enhancing public safety.* Washington, DC: Urban Institute.

Lawrence, S., D.P. Mears, G. Dubin, and J. Travis. (2002). *The practice and promise of prison programming.* Washington DC: Urban Institute.

Le Blanc, M., and M. Fréchette. (1989). *Male criminal activity from childhood through youth: Multilevel and developmental perspectives.* New York: Springer-Verlag.

Lerman, R. (2002). *Marriage and the economic well-being of families with children: A review of the literature.* Report prepared for the U.S. Department of Health and Human Services, Office of the Assistant Secretary for Planning and Evaluation, Washington, DC. Available at http://www.urban.org/UploadedPDF/410541_LitReview.pdf (accessed March 2007).

Lindquist, C., J. Hardison, and P.K. Lattimore. (2003). *Reentry courts process evaluation (phase 1) final report.* Washington, DC: U.S. Department of Justice.

Lipsey, M. (1995). What do we learn from 400 research studies on the effectiveness of treatment with juvenile delinquents? In J. McGuire (Ed.), *What works: Reducing reoffending—guidelines from research and practice.* Chichester, England: Wiley.

Lipsey, M.W., G.L. Chapman, and N.A. Landenberger. (2001). Research findings from prevention and intervention studies: Cognitive-behavioral programs for offenders. *Annals of the American Academy of Political and Social Science, 578*, 144-157.

Lipsey, M.W., and F.T. Cullen. (2007). The effectiveness of correctional rehabilitation: A review of systematic reviews. *Annual Review of Law and Social Science, 3*.

Little, G.L. (2005). Meta-analysis of moral reconation therapy®: Recidivism results from probation and parole implementations. *Cognitive-Behavioral Treatment Review, 14*, 14-16.

Lochner, L., and E. Moretti. (2004). The effect of education on crime: evidence from prison inmates, arrests, and self-reports. *American Economic Review, 94*, 155-189.

Loeber, R., and M. LeBlanc. (1990).Towards a developmental criminology. In M. Tonry and N Morris (Eds.), *Crime and justice: A review of research* (vol. 12, pp. 375-473). Chicago: University of Chicago Press.

Logan, C. (1993). Criminal justice performance measures for prisons. In *Performance measures for the criminal justice system: A collection of discussion papers for the BJS-Princeton Project.* Bureau of Justice Statistics (NCJ #143505). Washington, DC: U.S. Department of Justice.

Lombard, D., C. Krouse, K. Krouse, S. Pflueger, and S. Hudson. (2004). *Allen County reentry: 2 year pilot study.* Available at http://allencountycorrections.com/2YRReport.pdf [accessed Oct. 2007].

Lurigio, A. (2001). Effective services for parolees with mental illness. *Crime and Delinquency, 47*, 446-461.

Lynch, J.P., and W. Sabol. (2001). Prisoner reentry in perspective. *Urban Institute Crime Policy Report.* Washington, DC: Urban Institute.

MacKenzie, D.L. (2006). *What works in corrections?* Cambridge Studies in Criminology. New York: Cambridge University Press.

Maguire, K. (1994). *Sourcebook of criminal justice statistics, 1993.* Washington DC: U.S. Bureau of Justice Statistics and Albany, NY: Micheal J. Hindelang Criminal Justice Research Center.

Maltz, M.D. (1984). *Recidivism.* Orlando, FL: Academic Press. Available at http://www.uic.edu/depts/lib/ (accessed July 2007).

Manza, J., and C. Uggen. (2006). *Locked out: Felon disenfranchisement and American democracy.* New York: Oxford University Press.

Marlowe, D. (2003). Drug policy by popular referendum: This, too, shall pass. *Journal of Substance Abuse Treatment, 25,* 213-221.

Marlowe, D.B. (2006). When "what works" never did: Dodging the "scarlet m" in correctional rehabilitation. *Criminology and Public Policy, 5,* 339-346.

Martinson, R. (1974). What works? Questions and answers about prison reform. *The Public Interest, 35,* 22-54.

Maruna, S. (2001). *Making good: How ex-offenders reform and reclaim their lives.* Washington, DC: American Psychological Association.

Maruna, S., and T. LeBel. (2003). Welcome home? Examining the "reentry court" concept from a strengths-based perspective. *Western Criminology Review, 4*(2), 91-107.

Maume, M.O., G.C. Ousey, and K. Beaver. (2005). Cutting the grass: A reexamination of the link between marital attachment, delinquent peers, and desistance from marijuana use. *Journal of Quantitative Criminology, 21,* 27-53.

McCleary, R. (1992). *Dangerous men: The sociology of parole.* New York: Harrow and Heston.

Metraux, S., and D.P. Culhane. (2004). Homeless shelter use and reincarceration following prison release: Assessing the risk. *Criminology and Public Policy, 3,* 201-222.

Monahan, J., and H. Steadman. (1994). *Crime and mental disorder.* Washington, DC: U.S. Department of Justice, National Institute of Justice.

Mumola, C.J. (2000). *Incarcerated parents and their children.* (Bureau of Justice Statistics Special Report.) Washington, DC: U.S. Department of Justice.

Mumola, C.J., and J.C. Karberg. (2006). *Drug use and dependence, state and federal prisoners, 2004.* Bureau of Justice Statistics (NCJ #213530). Washington, DC: U.S. Department of Justice. Available at http://www.ojp.usdoj.gov/bjs/abstract/dudsfp04.htm (accessed February 2007).

Nagin, D.S., A.R. Piquero, E. Scott, and L. Steinberg. (2006). Public preferences for rehabilitation versus incarceration of juvenile offenders: Evidence from a contingent valuation survey. *Criminology and Public Policy, 5*(4), 627-651.

Nagin, D.S., and R. Paternoster. (1994). Personal capital and social control: The deterrence implications of individual differences in criminal offending. *Criminology, 32,* 581-606.

Nagin, D., and J. Waldfogel. (1998).The effect of conviction on income through the life cycle. *International Review of Law and Economics, 18,* 25-40.

National Institute of Justice. (2006). *Drug courts: The second decade.* Special report (NCJ #211081). Washington DC: U.S. Department of Justice.

National Institute on Drug Abuse. (2006). *Principles of drug abuse treatment for criminal justice populations—A research-based guide.* Available at http://www.nida.nih.gov/PODAT_CJ/ (accessed October 2006).

National Research Council. (1979). *The rehabilitation of criminal offenders: Problems and prospects.* Panel on Research on Rehabilitative Techniques, S.E. Martin, L.B. Sechrest, and R. Redner (Eds.). Committee on Research on Law Enforcement and the Administration of Justice. Washington, DC: National Academy Press.

National Research Council. (1986). *Criminal careers and career criminals volume 1.* A. Blumstein, J. Cohen, J.A. Roth, and C.A. Visher, Eds. Panel on Research on Criminal Careers, Committee on Research on Law Enforcement and the Administration of Justice. Commission on Behavioral and Social Sciences and Education. Washington, DC: National Academy Press.

National Research Council. (2005). *Improving evaluation of anticrime programs.* M.W. Lipsey (Ed.), Committee on Improving Evaluation of Anti-Crime Programs. Committee on Law and Justice, Division of Behavioral and Social Sciences and Education. Washington, DC: The National Academies Press.

Nelson. M., P. Deess, and C. Allen. (1999). *The first month out: Post-incarceration experiences in New York City.* New York: Vera Institute of Justice.

Northwest Law Enforcement and Public Safety Training. (2006). *Conference proceedings.* Available at http://www.nwleconference.com/tracks.htm (accessed March 2007).

Office of Justice Programs. (1999). *Reentry courts: Managing the transition from prison to community. A call for concept papers.* Washington, DC: U.S. Department of Justice.

Olson, B.D., L.A. Jason, J.R. Ferrari, and T.D. Hutcheson. (2005). Bridging professional- and mutual-help through a unifying theory of change: An application of the transtheoretical model to the mutual-help organization. *Journal of Applied and Preventative Psychology, 11,* 168-178.

Osgood, D.W., and H. Lee. (1993). Leisure activities, age, and adult roles across the lifespan. *Society and Leisure 16,* 181-208.

Osgood, D.W., J.K. Wilson, P.M. O'Malley, J.G. Bachman, and L.D. Johnston. (1996). Routine activities and individual deviant behavior. *American Sociological Review 61,* 635-655.

Pager, D. (2003). The mark of a criminal record. *American Journal of Sociology, 108,* 937-975.

Pager, D., and L. Quillian. (2005). Walking the talk: What employers do versus what they say. *American Sociological Review, 70,* 355-380.

Pearson, F., and D.S. Lipton. (1999). A meta-analytic review of the effectiveness of corrections-based treatments for drug abuse. *Prison Journal, 79*(4), 384-410.

Petersilia, J. (1999). Parole and prisoner reentry in the United States. *Crime and Justice, 26,* 479-529.

Petersilia, J. (2001). *Reforming probation and parole in the 21st century.* Washington, DC: American Correctional Association.

Petersilia, J. (2003). *When prisoners come home: Parole and prisoner reentry.* New York: Oxford University Press.

Petersilia, J. (2004). What works in prisoner reentry? Reviewing and questioning the evidence. *Federal Probation, 68*(2), 4-8.

Petersilia, J. (2005). From cell to society: Who is returning home? In J. Travis and C. Visher (Eds.), *Prisoner reentry and crime in America* (pp. 15-49). New York: Cambridge University Press.

Petersilia, J. (2006). *Understanding California corrections.* California Policy Research Center, University of California, Berkeley. Available at http://www.ucop.edu/cprc/document/understand_ca_corrections.pdf (accessed February 2007).

Petersilia, J., and S. Turner. (1993). Intensive probation and parole. In M. Tonry (Ed.), *Crime and justice: An annual review of research.* Chicago: University of Chicago Press.

Pew Charitable Trusts. (2007). *Public safety, public spending: Forecasting America's prison population 2007-2011*. Prepared by the JFA Institute for the Public Safety Performance Project. Available at http://www.pewpublicsafety.org/pdfs/PCT%20Public%20Safety%20Public%20Spending.pdf (accessed June 2007).

Pezzin, L.E. (1995). Earning prospects, matching effects, and the decision to terminate a criminal career. *Journal of Quantitative Criminology*, 11, 29-50.

Piehl, A.M. (1998). Economic conditions, work, and crime. In M. Tonry (Ed.), *Handbook on crime and punishment* (pp. 302-319). New York: Oxford University Press.

Piquero, A.R. (2004). Somewhere between persistence and desistance: The intermittency of criminal careers. In S. Maruna and R. Immarigeon (Eds.), *After crime and punishment: Pathways to offender re-integration* (pp. 102-125). New South Wales: Federation Press.

Piquero, A.R., J.M. MacDonald, and K.F. Parker. (2002). Race, local life circumstances, and criminal activity. *Social Science Quarterly*, 83, 654-670.

Piquero, A.R., and G. Pogarsky. (2002). Beyond Stafford and Warr's reconceptualization of deterrence: Personal and vicarious experiences, impulsivity, and offending behavior. *Journal of Research in Crime and Delinquency*, 39(2), 153-186.

Quinn, J.F., and L.A. Gould. (2003). The prioritization of treatment among Texas parole officers. *The Prison Journal*, 83(3), 323-336.

Raphael, S., and M.A. Stoll (2004). The effect of prison releases on regional crime rates. *Brookings-Wharton Papers on Urban Affairs*, 5, 207-255.

Rapp-Paglicci, L.A., and A. Roberts. (2004). Mentally ill juvenile offenders. In A. Roberts (Ed.), *Juvenile justice sourcebook, 2nd edition*. New York: Oxford University Press.

Rhine, E.E., T.L. Mawhorr, and E.C. Parks. (2006). Implementation: The bane of effective correctional programs. *Criminology and Public Policy*, 5, 347-358.

Roman, C., and J. Travis. (2004). *Taking stock: Housing, homelessness, and prisoner reentry*. Washington, DC: Urban Institute.

Roman, J. (2005). Are drug courts a solution to the drug problem? Comment at the Urban Institute Conference on April 5. Available at http://www.urban.org/publications/900803.html (accessed November 2006).

Rosenfeld, R., J. Wallman, and R. Fornango. (2005). The contribution of ex-prisoners to crime rates. In J. Travis and C. Visher (Eds.), *Prisoner reentry and crime in America* (pp. 80-104). New York: Cambridge University Press.

Rossi, P.H., R.A. Berk, and K.J. Lenihan. (1980). *Money, work, and crime: Experimental evidence*. New York: Academic Press.

Rossman, S.B., and C.G. Roman. (2003). Case managed reentry and employment: Lessons from the Opportunity to Succeed Program. *Justice Research and Policy*, 5(2), 75-100.

Sampson, R.J., and J.H. Laub. (1990). Crime and deviance over the life course: The salience of adult social bonds. *American Sociological Review*, 55, 609-627.

Sampson, R.J., and J.H. Laub. (1993). *Crime in the making: Pathways and turning points through life*. Cambridge, MA: Harvard University Press.

Sampson, R.J., and J.H. Laub. (2003). Desistance from crime over the life course. In J.T. Mortimer and M.J. Shanahan (Eds.), *Handbook of the life course* (pp. 295-310). New York: Kluwer Academic/Plenum.

Sampson, R.J., J.H. Laub, and C. Wimer. (2006). Does marriage reduce crime? A counterfactual approach to within-individual causal effects. *Criminology*, 44, 465-508.

Sampson, R.J., S. Raudenbush, and F. Earls. (1999). Neighborhoods and violent crime: A multilevel study of collective efficacy. *Science*, 277, 918-924.

Schma, W.G. (2000). Judging for the new millennium. *Court Review*, 37(1), 4-6.

Schmidt, P., and A. Witte. (1988). *Predicting recidivism using survival models*. New York: Springer-Verlag.

Seiter, R.P., and K.R. Kadela. (2003). Prisoner reentry: What works, what does not, and what is promising. *Crime and Delinquency, 49*(3), 360-388.

Shapiro, C. (2003). The Bodega model: A family focused approach for returning prisoners. *The Source, 12*(1) (Spring). Available at http://www.familyjustice.org/assets/publications/The_Bodega_Model.pdf (accessed February 2007).

Shaw, C.R., and H.D. McKay. (1969). *Juvenile delinquency in urban areas, revised edition.* Chicago: University of Chicago Press.

Shover, N. (1996). *Great pretenders: Pursuits and careers of persistent thieves.* Boulder, CO: Westview Press.

Skinner, B.F. (1974). *About behaviorism.* New York: Random House.

Solomon, A., V. Kachnowski, and A. Bhati. (2005). *Does parole work? Analyzing the impact of postprison supervison on rearrest outcomes.* Washington, DC: Urban Institute.

Stall, R., and P. Biernacki. (1986). Spontaneous remission from the problematic use of substances: An inductive model derived from a comparative analysis of the alcohol, opiate, tobacco, and food/obesity literatures. *International Journal of the Addictions, 21*, 1-23.

Stillman, J. (1999). *Working to learn: Skills development under work first.* Philadelphia: Public/Private Ventures.

Sullivan, E., M. Mino, K. Nelson, and J. Pope. (2002). *Families as a resource in recovery from drug abuse: An evaluation of La Bodega de la Familia.* New York: Vera Institute of Justice.

Taxman, F. (1998). *Reducing recidivism through a seamless system of care: Components of effective treatment, supervision, and transition services in the community.* College Park, MD: U.S. Office of National Drug Control Policy.

Taxman, F. (2006). *A behavioral management approach to supervision: Preliminary findings from Maryland's Proactive Community Supervision (PCS) pilot program.* Paper prepared for the Workshop on Community Supervision and Desistance from Crime, Committee on Law and Justice, National Research Council. Available from L. Douglas Wilder School of Government and Public Affairs, Virginia Commonwealth University.

Tonry, M. (2004). *Thinking about crime: Sense and sensibility in American penal culture.* New York: Oxford University Press.

Travis, J. (2000). *But they all come back: Rethinking prisoner reentry.* Research in Brief, Sentencing and Corrections: Issues for the 21st Century. National Institute of Justice. Washington, DC: U.S. Department of Justice. Available at http://www.ncjrs.gov/pdffiles1/nij/181413.pdf (accessed November 2006).

Travis, J. (2005). *But they all come back: Facing the challenges of prisoner reentry.* Washington, DC: Urban Institute Press.

Uggen, C. (2000). Work as a turning point in the life course of criminals: A duration model of age, employment, and recidivism. *American Sociological Review, 65*, 529-546.

Uggen, C., and J. Manza. (2004). Voting and subsequent crime and arrest: Evidence from a community sample. *Columbia Human Rights Law Review, 36*, 193-216.

Uggen, C., J. Manza, and A. Behrens. (2004). Less than the average citizen, stigma, role transition and the civic reintegration of convicted felons. In S. Maruna and R. Immarigeon (Eds.), *After crime and punishment: Pathways to offender reintegration* (pp. 258-290). Cullompton, Devon, England: Willan.

Uggen, C., and M. Massoglia. (2003). Desistance from crime and deviance as a turning point in the life course. In J.T. Mortimer and M.J. Shanahan (Eds.), *Handbook of the life course* (pp. 311-329). New York: Kluwer Academic/Plenum.

U.S. Department of Health and Human Services. (2004). *What can we say about the effectiveness of jail diversion programs for persons with co-occurring disorders?* TAPA Center for Jail Diversion, National GAINS Center, Substance Abuse and Mental Health Services Administration. Available at http://www.nicic.org/Library/020010 (accessed October 2006).

U.S. Department of Health and Human Services. (2007). *Healthy marriage initiative.* Available at http://www.acf.hhs.gov/healthymarriage/ (accessed July 2007).

U.S. Government Accountability Office. (2005). *Adult drug courts: Evidence indicates recidivism reductions and mixed results for other outcomes.* (GAO-05-219.) Washington, DC: Author.

Visher, C. (2006). Editorial introduction: Effective reentry programs. *Criminology and Public Policy,* 5, 299-302.

Visher, C., and S. Courtney. (2006). *Cleveland prisoners' experiences returning home.* Washington, DC: Urban Institute. Available at http://www.urban.org/url.cfm?ID=311359 (accessed September 2006).

Visher, C., and J. Farrell. (2005). *Chicago communities and prisoner reentry.* Washington, DC: Urban Institute.

Visher, C., V. Kachnowski, N. La Vigne, and J. Travis. (2004). *Baltimore prisoners' experiences returning home.* Washington, DC: Urban Institute Press.

Visher, C., N. La Vigne, and J. Farrell. (2003). *Illinois prisoners' reflections on returning home.* Washington, DC: Urban Institute Press.

Visher, C., and K. Mallik-Kane. (2007). Reentry experiences of men with health problems. In R. Greifinger (Ed.), *Public health is public safety: Improving public health through correctional health care.* New York: Springer-Verlag.

Visher, C.A., R. Naser, and S. Courtney. (2007). Incarcerated fathers: Pathways from prison to home. In V.S. Gadsen and P. Genty (Eds.) *Incarcerated parents, their children, and their families.* Mahwah, NJ: Lawrence Erlbaum.

Visher C.A., L. Winterfield, and M.B. Coggeshall. (2005). Ex-offender employment programs and recidivism: A meta-analysis. *Journal of Experimental Criminology,* 1(3), 295-315.

Waldron, H.B., and Y. Kaminer. (2004). On the learning curve: The emerging evidence supporting cognitive-behavioral therapies for adolescent substance abuse. *Society for the Study of Addiction,* 99, 93-105.

Waite, L.J., and M. Gallagher. (2000). *The case for marriage: Why married people are happier, healthier, and better off financially.* New York: Random House.

Walker, J.S., and E.J. Bruns. (2003). Quality and fidelity in Wraparound. *Focal Point: A national journal on family support and children's mental health,* 17, 21-23.

Walker, J.S., and E.J. Bruns. (2006). Building on practice-based evidence: Using expert perspectives to define the wraparound process. *Psychiatry Services,* 57, 1579-1585.

Warr, M. (1998). Life-course transitions and desistance from crime. *Criminology,* 36, 183-216.

Weibush, R.G., B. McNulty, and T. Le. (2000). *Implementation of the intensive community-based aftercare program.* Bulletin, Office of Justice Programs, Office of Juvenile Justice and Delinquency Prevention. Washington, DC: U.S. Department of Justice.

Weibush, R.G., D. Wagner, B. McNulty, Y. Wang, and T.N. Le. (2005). *Implementation and outcome evaluation of the intensive aftercare program: Final report.* (NCJ 206177). Available at http://www.ncjrs.gov/pdffiles1/ojjdp/206177.pdf [accessed Oct. 2007].

Weitekamp, E.G.M., and H.-J. Kerner. (1994). Epilogue: Workshop and plenary discussions, and future directions. In E.G.M. Weitekamp and H-J.Kerner (Eds.), *Cross-national longitudinal research on human development and criminal behavior* (pp. 439-449). Dordrecht, The Netherlands: Kluwer Academic.

Wexler, H.K. (1995). The success of therapeutic communities for substance abusers in American prisons. *Journal of Psychoactive Drugs, 27,* 57-66.

Wilkinson, R. (2004). *Reentry best practices: Directors' perspectives.* Middletown, CT: The Association of State Correctional Administrators.

Wilkinson, R., and G.A. Bucholtz. (2003). *Prison reform through offender reentry: A partnership between courts and corrections.* Paper prepared for Pace Law School Symposium on Prison Reform Law, October 2003. Available at http://www.drc.state.oh.us/web/Articles/article93.htm (accessed November 2006).

Wilson, D., C. Gallagher, and D. MacKenzie. (2000). A meta-analysis of corrections-based education, vocation, and work programs for adult offenders. *Journal of Research in Crime and Delinquency, 37,* 347-368.

Wilson, J.A., and R.C. Davis. (2006). Good intentions meet hard realities: An evaluation of the Project Greenlight Reentry Program. *Criminology and Public Policy, 5,* 303-338.

Wilson, J.Q. (2002). *The marriage problem: How our culture has weakened families.* New York: HarperCollins.

Wilson, J.Q., and G.L. Kelling. (1982). Broken windows: The police and neighborhood safety. *Atlantic Monthly* (March), 29-38.

Winterfield, L., and J. Castro. (2005). *Returning home Illinois policy brief: Treatment matching.* Washington, DC: Urban Institute. Available at http://www.urban.org/url.cfm?ID=311216 (accessed September 2006).

Witten, L. (2006). Medications Development Division nurtures the creation of new addiction treatments. *NIDA at Work, 20*(6)(July).

Zhang, S., R.E.L. Roberts and V.J. Callanan. (2006). Preventing parolees from returning to prison through community-based reintegration. *Crime and Delinquency, 52*(4) 551-571.

Appendix A

Workshop Agenda

WEDNESDAY, JANUARY 18, 2006

8:30–8:45 am **WELCOMING REMARKS AND INTRODUCTIONS**
Carol Petrie, Director
Committee on Law and Justice

James Q. Wilson, Committee Chair
Emeritus, University of California Los Angeles

8:45–9:05 Issues in Reentry Research for NIJ
Glenn Schmitt (invited)
Acting Director, NIJ

9:05–9:30 Overview of Issues and Workshop Goals
Joan Petersilia
Committee on Community Supervision and Desistance from Crime
University of California, Irvine

9:30–11:00	**Community Supervision Current Practice**
	From: Rethinking Rehabilitation: Why Can't We Reform Our Criminals David Farabee University of California Los Angeles
	Discussants: Michael Jacobsen, Executive Director Vera Institute of Justice
	Martin Horn, Commissioner New York City Department of Corrections
	General Discussion
11:00–11:15	Break
11:15–12:45 pm	**Therapeutic Models of Community Supervision**
	Efficacy of the Proactive Model of Supervision Faye Taxman Virginia Commonwealth University
	Discussants: Shadd Maruno Queens College, Belfast
12:45–1:30	Lunch
1:30–3:00	**Reentry: The Judicial Model**
	The Role of Problem Solving Courts David B. Wexler J.D. University of Arizona and University of Puerto Rico
	Discussants:
	Hon Cindy Lederman, Administrative Judge Eleventh Judicial Circuit Juvenile Division Miami-Dade County, Florida

Jennifer Skeem (invited)
UC Irvine

General Discussion

3:00–3:15   **Break**

3:15–4:30   **The Way Forward**

What Would an Ideal System Look Like?
Pamela Lattimore
University of South Carolina

Discussants:
Mark Kleiman
University of California, Los Angeles

Sharon Neumann, Deputy Director
Oklahoma Department of Corrections

4:30–5:00   **Wrap-Up**

Jeremy Travis, President
John Jay College
New York, NY

5:00   **Adjourn**

Appendix B

Biographical Sketches of Committee Members and Staff

Joan Petersilia (*Cochair*) is a professor of criminology, law, and society in the School of Social Ecology and director of the Center for Evidence-Based Corrections at the University of California at Irvine. Previously, she was director of the criminal justice program at RAND and has directed major studies in policing, sentencing, career criminals, juvenile justice, corrections, and racial discrimination. Her current work focuses on parole and prisoner reintegration. She has served as president of both the American Society of Criminology and of the Association of Criminal Justice Research in California, and she is an elected fellow of both the American Society of Criminology and the National Academy of Public Administration. She has a B.A. degree in sociology from Loyola University, an M.A. degree in sociology from Ohio State University, and a Ph.D. in criminology from the University of California at Irvine.

Richard Rosenfeld (*Cochair*) is professor of criminology and criminal justice at the University of Missouri-St. Louis. He is coauthor with Steven F. Messner of *Crime and the American Dream* (Wadsworth) and has written extensively on the social sources of violent crime. His current research focuses on the effects of economic conditions on crime trends. Rosenfeld is a fellow of the American Society of Criminology.

Richard J. Bonnie is John S. Battle professor of law, professor of psychiatric medicine, and director of the Institute of Law, Psychiatry, and Public Policy at the University of Virginia. His work focuses on criminal law and law relating to mental health, substance abuse, and public health. His many public service activities have included serving as secretary of the first National Advisory Council on Drug Abuse, chair of Virginia's State Human Rights Committee, and, currently, chair of the Commission on Mental Health Law Reform established by the chief justice of Virginia. Bonnie is a recipient of the Ray Award of the American Psychiatric Association and a special presidential commendation for his contributions to American psychiatry. He is a member of the Institute of Medicine of the National Academies and received its Yarmolinsky Medal for his contributions to the institution.

Robert D. Crutchfield is professor and Clarence and Elissa Schrag fellow in the Department of Sociology at the University of Washington. His current research focuses on social inequality as a cause of crime and racial inequality in the criminal justice system. Prior to his academic career, he was a juvenile probation officer and an adult parole officer in Pennsylvania. He also served on the Washington State Juvenile Sentencing Commission. He is a past vice president of the American Society of Criminology and is the coeditor of the third edition of *Crime: Readings*.

Eugenia Grohman (*Staff Officer*) is associate executive director of the Division of Behavioral and Social Sciences and Education at the National Research Council, with primary responsibility for the review, editing, publication, and release of the division's reports. She served as study director for the Panel on Data Access for Research Purposes for the last stages of its work, and she has worked on many division reports, including *Measuring Poverty: A New Approach*; *How People Learn*; *Understanding Risk*; *High Stakes: Testing for Tracking, Promotion, and Graduation*; and *A Common Destiny: Blacks and American Society*. Previously, she worked as a program and budget analyst in the federal government and in politics.

Mark A.R. Kleiman is professor of public policy at the School of Public Affairs of the University of California at Los Angeles where he teaches methods of policy analysis, and drug abuse and crime control policy. His primary research interests are drug abuse and crime control, with special attention to illicit markets and the design of deterrent regimes, and including simulation modeling of deterrence strategies and empirical work on the management of drug-involved offenders on probation and parole. Previously, he worked at the U.S. Department of Justice, the Office of Management and Budget for the city of Boston, the Polaroid Corporation, and for U.S. Representative Les Aspin. He is the author of *Marijuana: Costs of Abuse, Costs of Control* and *Against Excess: Drug Policy for Results*.

John H. Laub is professor in the Department of Criminology and Criminal Justice and an affiliate faculty member in the Department of Sociology at the University of Maryland and a visiting scholar at the Institute for Quantitative Social Science at Harvard University. He is a fellow of the American Society of Criminology and has served as its president, and in 2005 he received its Edwin H. Sutherland Award. His areas of research include crime and deviance over the life course, juvenile delinquency and juvenile justice, and the history of criminology. Two of his books, coauthored with Robert Sampson, *Crime in the Making: Pathways and Turning Points Through Life* and *Shared Beginnings, Divergent Lives: Delinquent Boys to Age 70*, have won several major awards.

Carol Petrie (*Study Director*) is director of the Committee on Law and Justice, a standing committee at the National Research Council. She develops and supervises a wide range of projects on the nature of crime and crime prevention and control. Previously, she was director of planning and management at the National Institute of Justice (NIJ) of the U.S. Department of Justice, working in the area of criminal justice research, statistics, and public policy. She was also a senior project officer at NIJ and served as its acting director in 1994. She has conducted research on violence and managed numerous research projects on the operations of the criminal justice system.

Christy A. Visher is principal research associate with the Justice Policy Center at the Urban Institute in Washington, D.C. Previously, she was science adviser to the director of the National Institute of Justice, the research arm of the U.S. Department of Justice. Her research focuses on criminal careers, communities and crime, and the evaluation of strategies for crime control and prevention. She is coeditor with Jeremy Travis of *Prisoner Reentry and Crime in America* and the author of several recent publications on prisoner reintegration.